The dangers of the Internet

On the end of female and also of male intuition

Cacildo Marques

ISBN: **979-8649141147**

Cover: Clouds

Episteme Ed

Marques, Cacildo

The dangers of the Internet: On the end of female and also of male intuition./ Maryland, 2020.

108p.

ISBN: **979-8649141147**

1. Internet. I. Title

DDC 004.678

The dangers of the Internet

On the end of female and also of male intuition

Cacildo Marques

CONTENT

Preface

Analog and digital are two worlds in one

Is there an extension of your physical body beyond your immediate surroundings, beyond the range of carbon-14 emissions from your bones?

When you open the glass door of the shopping center from the luminous substance pouring from your skin, you have the proof that you act remotely, through the photoelectric effect. Does it stop there?

What this book says is that it doesn't. In addition to stating that the "lamp of your body" transcends the limits of your steps, it analyzes the two modes of expansion of the particles carried by this wave of light: The analog and the digital.

The differences between them are of astronomical dimensions, to the point that we can understand the advent of bits as a watershed in history. They were conceived by Leibniz, in the 17th century; transformed into the possibility of electronic configuration by Charles Sanders Peirce, in 1896; shaped into a machine by Konrad Zuse, in 1936; and deepened in theoretical works by Claude Shannon in the same year, in a master's thesis considered the most important in the history, which consolidated the basis that allowed the development of the commercial computer bore on the ideas of Turing (also from 1936), the coordination of John von Neumann at ENIAC, in 1946, and the manufacture of UNIVAC I by John Eckert and John Mauchly, in 1951. This history is remembered in more detail in the text.

Six decades later, because of the Internet and the miniaturization of the computer in smartphones, the world of bits has become part of the lives of citizens, who have started to carry it in their pockets in all the municipalities on the Earth.

In June 2016, after the result of the Brexit referendum, academia, the press and governments began to discuss this new reality, which is the power that digital communication exercises over people's decision. However, since the end of the 20th century, many scholars have recognized the depth of change. The novelty, from the last century to these days, is that not only are some people involved in the experiment, as before, but almost all human beings.

For 17 years I taught computer programming for young people, having learned a lot about how people idealize, fear or decipher the computer and, in more recent times, the Internet. This present book, although it does not teach programming, was written as a continuation of the messages that I always tried to take to users of the computer keyboards, now also users of the cloud.

Just as many have opened my eyes, my idea here is to help open yours, if I can count on your good will.

Cacildo Marques, S. Paulo, May, 2020.

Chapter 1. Communication with the machine

No one is in any doubt as to the greatness of the revolution that the Internet has meant within the evolution of machines, since Blaise Pascal, in 1642, designed his crank calculator to perform sums.

Years ago, in a lecture in Sao Paulo, a professor said that the three great technological steps in human history are the inventions of the wheel, the writing and the Internet.

He was not someone in the area of Computing or Engineering, because they know that the Internet is an incremental advance, joining information technology and telecommunications, much more than a great leap in technical progress by itself.

Let us see. Before the launch of the net, which is the great consolidation www (World Wide Web), on January 23, 1991, many intermediate projects seeking to connect computers worldwide were tried. In 1961, researcher Leonard Kleinrock, from MIT, published an article exposing the idea of (data) packet switching, not just of circuits. In 1962 psychologist J. C. R. Licklider, also from MIT, started to defend and spread the idea of "networking", with the use of computers, and launched his proposal for a "galactic network". His plan was for researchers at ARPA (Advanced Research Projects Agency) to embrace that purpose. ARPA had been created in 1957, by the United States Department of Defense, with a view to ensuring the country's prominence in the development and use of high technology in the military.

Mail. When did e-mail start?

In 1969 ARPA launched Arpanet, an e-mail (electronic mail) communication system, using the NCP (Network Control Protocol), which in 1981 was divided into TCP (Transmission Control Protocol) and IP (Internet Protocol). Many years before that, inventor Nikola Tesla (1856-1943) published articles with predictions about what electricity and wireless communication could do for humanity. He predicted that telephone stations around the world would be connected, allowing news, photographs and texts to be broadcast.

Grace Murray Hopper made the first compiler

There seems to be a missing link in this story. How does the human element communicate with the computer, making it communicate with another human being? But the link is not lost. In 1952 Grace Murray Hopper, professor of Mathematics at Harvard University, developed the A-0 language, creating the first compiler of computer programs. With that, she started a revolutionary idea, which was to exchange the model of sending communication to the machine using the codes of the machine itself for the new programming model with human words, in what came to be called "high-level language", as opposed to the "machine language". Instead of using a strange numeric or alphanumeric code, which the machine "interpreted" in its bits (zeros and ones, or off-on) as being the order "multiply", it would now suffice to write on the keyboard the word "multiply"(some years before, Konrad Zuse, in Germany, walked a little in this purpose of sending human words to the machine, but Hopper gave the final and functional form to the project). The machine was then in charge of translating this human command into its binary sequences. This feat of 1952 represented a watershed in the history of computing.

Tesla's glimpse was present in the creation of the Telex, in 1926, popularized later in the Fax machine, used for sending texts and other data via the telephone line, until he was retired at the end of the 20th century. When joining the idea of Telex with the communication between man and the computer via human language, according to Professor Grace's inventions, we arrived at Arpanet and, from there, on the Internet.

Chapter 2. The computer

With computers and telephone exchanges to which the so-called "electronic brains" could be connected, it was not difficult for mathematicians and engineers of the 1950s to devise a system for transferring data between machines located in different cities or even distant countries. At that same time, artificial satellites were being developed, and they would further include in their family these members now known as communication satellites, which facilitated the connection between machines around the world.

Center. Did the computer have an inventor?
Telephone wires and, later, satellites are important elements in the history of the Internet, but the central figure in all this is the computer, without a doubt. It is an invention that has developed over three centuries. To make a comparison, in 1804 the British engineer Richard Trevithick put a steam engine to travel on iron tracks and with that he invented the train, the first locomotive, two decades before George Stephenson have built the first commercial railway. The train therefore has had its undisputed inventor in Trevithick. The history of the computer is much more complex.
From Blaise Pascal's adding machine, Pascalina (1642), to ENIAC (1946), by John von Neumann's team, there were many crucial steps. We cannot reasonably understand how the computer works if we do not go through these steps.

Pascalina. Who invented the multiplication machine?
Étienne, Blaise Pascal's father, was an income inspector, and often lost nights of sleep by candlelight, accounting for taxes already levied and those he still had to collect. It distressed young Blaise, who once had the idea of building a machine to add and decrease, which his father could use in his work. Some businessmen were interested and ordered new units of the machine from Pascal, who made 50 of them. One copy still exists and belongs to the IBM museum in New York State.
In 1671, therefore, 19 years after Pascal's invention, Leibniz

went further and added to the Pascalina the multiplication and division functions, in a new machine called Stepped Reckoner, which also included the ability to extract square root.

Binary. Did Leibniz make more inventions in this field?

Among his various inventions, Leibniz also created the Binary Arithmetic, or Base 2 Arithmetic, the one of the zeros and ones that modern computers use, but he could not envision the use of this invention in the calculator, so that countless manufacturers, from that phase, launched in the market many models of Stepped Reckoner calculating machines, always based on the decimal arithmetic model, and that was the case until 1972, when the electronic pocket calculators, equipped with a liquid crystal screen, were placed for sale, developed by technicians of the RCA company in the previous decade.

Leibniz sensed that his Binary Arithmetic would be of great utility, but he was unable to find out what it was in his lifetime. (If we want to write, for example, the number 13, in base 2, we take the successive remains of the divisions by 2, which will be just zeros and ones. We do 13:2, which gives 6 with remainder One; then 6:2, which gives 3 with remainder Zero, then 3:2, which gives 1 with remainder One, and finally 1:2, which gives 0 with remainder One. Now we take this sequence of remains from the end to the beginning: One-One-Zero-One. The number 13 on a binary basis is 1101. If we read the binary number - which is what the binary computer does electronically - the sequence 1101, how do we know that this represents the number 13 in our decimal base? It's easy. We write the number in polynomial form, already in base 10: $1*2^3 + 1*2^2 + 0*2^1 + 1*2^0$. This gives $8 + 4 + 0 + 1$, and we arrive in 13.)

Industrials had been making improvements to the Leibniz machine, successor to Pascalina, until that, half a century later, in 1822, an English manufacturer, Charles Babbage, developed a powerful calculator, which he called the "difference engine", capable of operating logarithm tables and solve polynomial functions.

Engine. Did Charles Babbage complete his big plan?

In 1833 Babbage started a more ambitious project, which was the creation of a machine that would do any type of calculation.

Since his plan was to solve even analytical functions, which are the functions of complex variables, he named the new invention as "analytical engine". He used the punch card reader of the Joseph Marie Jacquard's machine, which was previously used to inform the loom about patterns of prints on fabrics. In Babbage's new device, the cards would carry mathematical information. This punch card reading system continued to be used in large calculators and computers until the mid-1970s.

Babbage knew that his new machine was possible, but he could not see the mathematical resources that were still missing for it to work properly. After many years of unsuccessful attempt, the English government cut off the funding it had been providing the inventor to carry out the project. This is not where the computer was actually born.

Programmer. What advance did Babbage's machine unleash?

But his private student Ada Byron, Countess of Lovelace, daughter of the poet Lord Byron, when was invited to translate from the French the notes of a lecture he gave in Turin, Italy, about this machine that would become the computer, if it was ready, filled the work of footnotes explaining how the machine would solve certain problems raised there. Luigi Menabrea, an attentive young engineer who, watching the lecture, wrote it down point by point, later published all the work in French, and it was what Ada Byron translated. Those footnotes she created were machine-coded instructions. For this legacy, a century later, mathematicians recognized that she was the inventor of computer programming. In 1979, the Ada language, of the Algol (*Algorithm Language*, 1958) and Pascal (1970) family, was developed in the United States in his honor, such as the Pascal language had been also created as a well-deserved tribute to the inventor of the Pascalina.

Ada Byron, or Ada Lovelace, died in 1852 in her hometown, London, of uterine cancer, at the age of 36.

Ada Byron: First computer programmer

Tabulating. What role did Hollerith play in computing?

The idea of using punched cards to feed data to the analytical machine gained very practical use in the United States just over half a century after Babbage's lecture in Turin. In 1889, the young engineer Herman Hollerith, who had been working at the national patent office in Washington-DC since 1884, patented his auspicious Tabulating Machine, which was intended to tabulate statistical data read on punched cards. The 1890 census in the United States used this machine to give more precision and speed to work. That year, Hollerith endowed the machine with arithmetic operations, so that it would be used in accounting work. Punched cards, as well as punched ribbons, soon earned the name "hollerith", as well as the paycheck document itself, a name that remains in the 21st century.

Herman Hollerith founded the Tabulating Machine Company in 1896, to offer services not only to the government, but also to the private sector. At that time, one of the uses of Hollerith's machine was the correction of competition tests, in the sadly famous multiple-choice questions. In 1911 his brand merged with three other companies in the technological field, forming the Computing Tabulating Recording Corporation (CTR). In 1924 this company, already very powerful, gained a new name: International Business Machines Corporation (IBM). Herman Hollerith passed away in 1929 at the age of 69, leaving a monumental legacy in the history of computing, although he, like Babbage, did not actually build the computer itself.

Berlin. Where was the binary computer born?

Until the early 1930s, calculators worked internally with base-ten arithmetic, the same that we humans use when calculating with pencils. But in 1934 engineer Konrad Zuse, Leibniz's compatriot (important detail), a Berliner who worked for the German branch of Ford Motor Co., started to design his binary calculator, which he named Z1. He sought official funding, but the Nazi government did not trust the invention. He had to enlist the support of private companies to start building his machine, which took place between 1936 and 1938. It was, finally, a calculator built on a binary basis, the first in history, powered by data recorded on perforated tape, made of cellulose, which included programming, although still incipient.

This and other Zuse machines were destroyed by the bombings on Berlin in World War II, when he had already built the substitutes for that first, called Z2, Z3 and Z4. From 1943 to 1946 Zuse developed the Plankalkül language, for his machine that was left over from the war, the Z4, and today it is known that it was already a high-level language, although the project was only published in 1972.

Konrad Zuse's work represented a giant step towards obtaining the computer. All what remained now was to incorporate some mathematical advances that had been developed in England and the United States.

Algebra. Who created the Algebra of Logic?

In 1848, in England, George Boole published the book "Mathematical Analysis of Logic", in which he showed his development of an "Algebra" of Aristotle's Logic, expanding Leibniz's idea of the *calculus universalis*. In fact, that discipline that since Classical Greece was treated as a game of words, which represented propositions, or sentences, in their relations, was now expressed as an area of Mathematics, with its symbology and operations. In this "Algebra", Boole emphasized the role of the *And, Or* and *Not* connectives, which happened to be called logical connectives, or Boolean connectives.

This Boole Logic could have been the element that Babbage lacked for the completion of his Analytical Engine. But that was still not enough. In addition to needing to use Leibniz's Binary Arithmetic, Boole's Algebra itself would need another big step, which was done by the American logician Charles Sanders Peirce, son of mathematician Benjamin Peirce. As for Binary Arithmetic, Konrad Zuse came to use it in the following century, when he realized that he could electronically represent the values 0 and 1, certainly under the inspiration of Peirce's work, once 0 and 1 mean, under certain effect, *Not* and *Yes* (Yes = Denial of Not).

Connectives. How do you say "no" in electronics?

What Charles Sanders Peirce discovered in 1896 was that Boole's logical connectives could be represented in electrical, or electronic, circuits. The idea of *Not* is the simplest. When switching on the electrical circuit, which means sending a "yes", a switch turns off the current, which means answering "not". The idea of *And* is obtained with a circuit of two switch keys connected in series, _ \ _ \ _. When closing only one of the two keys, the first or the second, one does not have the passage of the current. For the current to pass, keeping the "yes", it is necessary to connect the two keys. If we have two sentences P and Q, it is not enough that only one of them is true for the composition P-and-Q to be true. Both must be true, that is, the two keys must be connected, allowing the current to flow. For example, (2 + 1 = 3) -and- (2 < 3) represents a true sentence, because it is a composition of two valid propositions. If we do (2 + 1 = 3) -and- (2> 3), we will have a false sentence, because one of the two propositions is a liar.

And how did young Peirce represent the connective *Or*? Since *And* is resolved in a series circuit, *Or* must be satisfied in a parallel circuit. In fact, with the two switch keys side by side, - <_> -, just connect one of the two switches, the top or the bottom, for the current to advance. If the top line is P and the bottom is Q, we can connect P-or-Q. If P is on (T) and Q is off (F), or if P is off (F) and Q is on (T), then the circuit is on (T). If we write (2 + 1 = 3) -or- (2

> 3), we will have a true sentence, even if evaluating one of the two propositions of the composition as false.

Digital. Was the 1944 IBM Mark I a computer?

Peirce had no way of experiencing his discovery on a concrete machine, because his ideas were on the head and on the sheet of paper. It was only in 1937 that electrical engineer and mathematician Claude Elwood Shannon, or simply Claude Shannon, of MIT (Massachusetts Institute of Technology), designed circuits for a digital calculator, using the creations of Babbage, Boole, Peirce and others. In 1941 he was able to test his invention at Bell Laboratories in New York. Shannon worked with Cryptography and is responsible for creating the Information Theory subject. In the computational sense, the word Bit was an idea of him, as a contraction of *binary digit*.

World War II came and efforts turned to the use of the large calculating machines that were already in the square.

In 1944 IBM sent to Harvard University the Mark I "analytical machine", built according to a project by Howard Aiken, which was inspired by Babbage's Analytical Machine. Mark I was just the nickname of the device officially called the IBM *Automatic Sequence Controlled Calculator* (IBM ASSC). As we can see, it was, admittedly, a calculator, still. Giant in size, it contained 760,000 sprockets and 800 kilometers of wire. This machine, still on a decimal basis, helped immensely in the war effort.

Code. How did Alan Turing contribute to Computing?

In the same way, and for the same time, English mathematician Alan Mathison Turing commanded a team of technicians in charge of deciphering the machine encryption used by the Nazis to determine times and locations of the bombings on England. This team worked at the military installations in the city of Buckingshire and used a calculator built in 1939, which they called "The Bombe".

With this rudimentary calculator, also base-ten, Alan Turing was able to decipher the Nazi bombing codes issued by the Enigma machine.

Years earlier, in 1936, Turing had been studying in the United States, at Princeton University, and there he lived with John von

Neumann, who would leave his mark on history for the next decade. There Turing wrote his remarkable article "On Computable Numbers", on which he developed a theoretical computer, later dubbed "paper computer", or "Turing machine". As it was a "paper" computer, it involved not electrical and electronic circuits, but only logical and numerical processes. One of the two long legs of the computer, the logical part, was configured there. The other leg, the electromechanical, belonged to the engineers. Computer Science is divided into *Software* (Computational Mathematics) and *Hardware* (physical structure of the computer).

In the following decades, the theoretical "Turing machine" started to be used as a test to verify whether a given machine is a computer or not. If it is a computer, it must do, logically, what the Turing machine would do.

As shown in the film "The Imitation Game", Turing would have to be presented as a national hero, deservedly, for his role in World War II. He was a homosexual and the practice of homosexuality was still prohibited in England. So he accepted, at the suggestion of government officials, to undergo hormonal treatment, to acquire manly posture. This hormone treatment was still unreliable at the time, and he died quickly. Officially, the narrative was consolidated that, distressed by the situation, he committed suicide, biting a poisoned apple.

Architecture. What does von Neumann architecture mean?

In 1945 mathematician John von Neumann published, along with other mathematicians and engineers, the text that defined what became known as "von Neumann architecture" for computers. It is a physical arrangement for the machine and its "peripherals". The machine itself comprises a set called *Central Processing Unit* (CPU), composed of an *Arithmetic Logic Unit* (ALU) and a *Control Unit*, with Memory beside it. The Control Unit contains a Program Counter and an Instruction Record. As peripherals, the machine has, on the one hand, the Input Device, and on the other, the Output Device.

Based on the von Neumann architecture, the first general purpose digital computer, the ENIAC (Electronic Numerical Integrator Automatic Computer), developed by John Presper Eckert and John William Mauchly, was completed and presented to the public on February 15, 1946, at the University of Pennsylvania. In operating mode, it was a tributary of the machine Z1 (1934), by Konrad Zuse, and Colossus (1944), by Tommy Flowers, designed in England under the guidance of Alan Turing to help decipher the Nazi codes of the Lorenz SZ40/42 machine. ENIAC was built by men, but its programming was in charge of six women: Betty Snyder Holberton, Jean Jennings Bartik, Kathleen McNulty Mauchly Antonelli, Marlyn Wescoff Meltzer, Ruth Lichterman Teltelbaum and Frances Bilas Spence. The machine occupied a space of 167 square meters, equivalent to a house of more than 8m in front by 20m in depth.

The von Neumann architecture was improved at Harvard by the so-called "Modified Harvard Architecture", which started to separate instruction memory and data memory. With that, machines started to have ROM (Read Only Memory), for instructions, RAM (Random Access Memory), for data, and flash memory, volatile auxiliary memory for data.

Many other types of computers were built at that stage, but the decisive step that led the machine into people's lives was the launch in March 1951 of the commercial computer UNIVAC I, built by the same duo from ENIAC, Eckert and Mauchly. Delivered the first unit for the census service in the United States, many more were being produced for engineering companies, banks, universities and so on.

Miniature. What crucial steps took place in 1982 and 1992?

In 1972, the Japanese company Sord Computer Corporation launched the first microcomputer, allowing citizens to have a computer on their desk. From 1975, with the launch of the Altair microcomputer, in the United States, the novelty has gained worldwide, with scale production and affordable prices.

In 1981 IBM launched the Personal Computer (PC), for use in offices, but it was not until the following year that the company introduced a model with a hard disk (HD). The machine was equipped with the DOS (Disk Operating System) and included programming through a version of the BASIC language (*Beginner's All-purpose Symbolic Instruction Code*) developed by Microsoft from an original version created by John Kemeny and Thomas Kurtz at Darmouth College, in 1964.

Also in 1981, Epson launched what is considered the first laptop in history, the Epson HX-20. Soon after this, executives had computers not only for use at their desks, but also for carrying in their briefcases and using on their laps.

The first smartphone, the Simon Personal Communicator, was also launched by IBM in 1992. Soon these machines would incorporate all the functions of a computer, and what in 1946 was the size of a large family house, came to fit in a box that the user carries in his pants pocket.

Chapter 3. The Internet

As mentioned above, the first communication by e-mail took place in 1969, between computers of the Department of Defense of the USA, in the Arpanet service, through the NCP protocol, root of the current TCP and IP protocols. In 1971 engineer Raymond (Ray) Tomlinson invented, at Arpanet, the e-mail "address", using the at sign (@).

The big step in communication between computers distant from each other was given in that moment, although that depended at the time on a telephone line.

The messages were made in plain text lines, without frames, without drawings, without photos.

Hypertext. What is the call from one text to another?

The Internet is, in fact, this communication between computers, but some new resources would have to be developed until the construction of the world web. One of the basic ideas had already been presented before Arpanet: hypertext. It is a concept identified by Ted Nelson, in 1965. A hypertext differs from an ordinary text because in that calls (links) are made to other texts or objects. When the Internet debuted in the 1990s, hypertext was already an old idea, but it needed to be programmed for its entry into on-network (online) communication.

Objects. Who created those little blocks on the screen?

The other big key to getting to the Internet was the Object Oriented Programming (OOP). The term is also old, created by Alan Kay in 1967, but the development of the technique came to light little by little, over the years. Alan Kay and some colleagues went on to work on the idea at Xerox, years later, using the 1980 Smalltalk language.

Alan Key: Programming for objects

Since Xerox's mission did not include selling computers or programs, those programmers who worked at the company called Steve Jobs, CEO of Apple Computer Inc, to introduce him to the news and see if he could market it. Jobs was a great inventor of machine models, but he was not a programmer. Then he called Bill Gates, Microsoft's CEO, with the intention of developing some joint project, of the two entrepreneurs.

Jobs was in for a big surprise months later. In 1981, Gates' Microsoft launched Windows 1.0, a program coupled to the DOS with colored windows on the screen, not just DOS text lines. These windows were the objects of the Xerox staff programming.

For the next ten years, Steve Jobs refused to speak to Bill Gates. The two talked again when Apple suffered a major crisis and needed loans to survive. Bill Gates stepped forward and offered a US$ 150 million contribution to his former friend's company. The offer was accepted and the two companies, Apple and Microsoft, remained independent, but economically sound. In this phase Apple developed its operating system based on objects, MacOS, from 1991.

Open. Did a free operating system come up?
Still in 1991, the young Finnish Linus Benedict Torvalds, a

software engineer based in the United States, launched a window program that was at the same time an operating system, the Linux. The big news is that this system is open source, admitting contributions from other programmers, in addition to being free. It is based on Unix, an operating system developed at Bell laboratories in 1969. Linux was inspired, although it was an independent development, in a previous Unix system, the Minix, created in 1987 by computer scientist Andrew Stuart Tanembaum.

It was only in 1993 that Microsoft launched a version of Windows that was the operating system itself, without relying on DOS, Windows NT 3.1, which became popular later in the version 3.5, as Windows 95. With competition from Linux, free, the prices of Windows versions after that time had to be reduced.

Services. In browsers and portals, who are the pioneers?

With operating systems based on windows (objects), the practice of hypertext already incorporated into tasks performed on a computer and sending and receiving of e-mail gaining ground, the world was ready for the arrival of the web, which happened, as we have seen above, in early 1991.

But the connections were slow and the data storage capacity was still very small. The facilities were gradually reaching users.

To visit the web pages of the existing portals, the user would need a friendly program. That is why the browser Netscape, free software from AOL (American On-Line), appeared in 1994. In its version 3 it included Netscape Composer, a window in which the user could program Internet pages.

In 1995, the search engine called Altavista appeared, as an extremely efficient research portal, given the limitations of its time. In 1996 Ask Jeeves, another search engine was designed to answer questions.

Also in 1996, the Hotmail e-mail service was launched on the market, offering free accounts. It was one of the first email services and was later purchased and incorporated by Microsoft.

The Yahoo portal (it is really an interjection, equivalent to Yay!), with its search service and its chat room, appeared in 1998. At the end of that same year the Google portal appeared (it is the name of a number, and means 10 powered to 100).

The first major social network was Myspace, launched in

2003 in Beverly Hills, California. It contained personal profiles, photos, music, user videos, chat room and groups. Later on, it incorporated an e-mail service and blogs. With the advancement of other social networks, Myspace has become a popular music portal.

In 2004, a social network with more facilities than Myspace, called Orkut, was created by a Google engineer named Orkut. For several years it was the greatest fun for young people on the Internet with regard to the interaction between friends, family and the so-called "virtual friends".

Smart. What novelty came from Facebook in 2008?

The smartphone has been trying to enter the world of the Internet with friendly platforms since its inception, despite its small size.

Several companies have undertaken to develop operating systems for these devices. Among these systems we had Android (2003), from Android Inc, and Windows CE (2005), from Microsoft. In 2005 Google bought Android Inc and invested in improving the product. In November 2007 the beta version of the new Android system was launched, and in September 2008 the functional version hit the market. If it were not for the iOS platform (2007), Apple's iPhone and iPad devices, Android would be in a monopoly condition, albeit free, given that competing systems practically fell into obscurity.

In 2008, year of the commercial launch of Google's Android, the social network Facebook, which on desktop computers and laptops was already burying Myspace and Orkut, launched its Facebook Phone version. Gradually, citizens in general were being attracted to possession of the smartphone, abandoning the old cell phone for simple phone calls, mainly because of access to Facebook. Many users, more than 50%, definitively abandoned the big computer to adopt exclusively an Android device, either cell phone or tablet.

As the social network, via Facebook, reached a large mass of users, human relations, including the practice of democracy, suffered a shock that they had not experienced since the proletarian revolutions of the beginning of the 20th century.

Chapter 4. The rise of flatearthists

The great results of science are not assimilated by the mass of individuals except through a certain educational effort. From the Mathematics of Tales, Pythagoras and Plato to the Biology of Lamarck, Edward Jenner, Darwin and Pasteur, through the Astronomy and the Physics of Copernicus, Galileo, Descartes, Huygens, Newton, Gauss and Maxwell, knowledge is brought to children and adolescents through hard training work, starting with literacy, without which all information is built without the most consistent basis.

Broadcasters. Is it possible to skip steps in learning?

Television, popularized since the 1950s, was already causing some discomfort in education, as it produced anxiety in children. While school needs a step-by-step, something that has been practiced since Pythagoras, for television it doesn't matter. Before the child learns about rotation and translation movements and about the force of gravity, essential notions for the absorption of information about the sphericity of the Earth, television has already told it that the Earth is a ball. It is information that, if it doesn't come at the right time, falls into the void. But the anxiety brought on by television comes from the fact that it advances information, while the teacher at school works with the sense of the simplest to the most complex, based on the idea of meaningful learning.

In the literacy phase, for example, the sentence is not required to be read before the child can read the words. And the words are not required to be read before the child learns the letters and syllables. This is the step-by-step way.

Contestation. Who does the flatearthist comfort himself with?

If television was already causing this disturbance, from top to bottom, the spread of Internet access, from 2008, brought the novelty of two-way. Information out of context and before the proper time now comes from top to bottom, bottom to top, left to right and right to left.

If previously there was disrespect to order in the transmission of knowledge, what happened to the popularized Internet was the contestation of information that requires the didactic steps of assimilation. Instead of absorbing the facts, using the necessary effort, the hurried person finds reinforcement in the interlocutor who faces the same problem. Teachers, scientists, journalists, artists and all those in charge of the responsible treatment of information saw, from one moment to the next, the accelerated growth of population groups that are adept at flatearthism, the rejection of vaccines, the disdain for health statistics and the denial of anthropogenic global warming.

Lies. Illiterates accept man walking on the moon?

Fake news had already been circulating through e-mail services before 2008, but that did not cause concern, because the users were people with a certain education and did not let the bullshit prosper. What appeared most frequently were apocryphal texts, which were chronicles written by anyone, but which gained a world by bringing false authorship by people like Albert Einstein, Clarice Lispector, Carl Sagan and others, always of great renown.

With the creation of YouTube in 2005, and its expansion from 2007, after being purchased by Google in October 2006, videos based on conspiracy "theories" went live, intermingling music posts, which have always formed the majority of videos from that portal. Among the most publicized were those that, with alleged evidence, denied the descent of man on the Moon.

Since then a new phenomenon has appeared on the scene: The emergence, in large numbers, of literate people denying the feat of Neil Armstrong, Edwin E. Aldrin Junior and Michael Collins, the three astronauts who descended on the Moon in July 1969, by the Apollo XI mission. Until then, only illiterate people, for very understandable reasons, refused to believe the fact. Literate people in this condition existed, but they were so rare that they never confessed disbelief. With the Internet, they started to feel comfortable in spreading their stupid incredulity.

Incredulous. Should we express any kind of doubt?

Doubting everything, as Descartes taught, is the basic and healthy attitude of the scientist. But the sense of ridicule also teaches the scientist to express doubts that are credible. For example, it is legitimate and reasonable to doubt the hypothesis that the dinosaurs were extinct because of the fall of the great meteor that formed the Gulf of Mexico. The great dinosaurs perished, but the small lizards and small birds are out there. The meteor-based explanation is accepted by most today, but it is controversial.

In contrast, doubting facts such as the derivation (quadrature) of the parabolic equation (Leibniz), the Theory of Gravitation (Newton), the role of oxygen in combustion (Lavoisier), the mechanism of Natural Selection (Darwin), the validity of the proof by Mathematical Induction (Peano), the functioning of the conditioned reflex (Pavlov) and the impossibility of long-term equilibrium by the invisible hand (Keynes), all this makes sense if the scientist's apprentice keeps the suspicion in his heart, without expressing it in conversations or in writing.

All of us who have been minimally educated have the duty to be unbelievers, but expressing disbelief regarding consolidated knowledge assimilable by all healthy-educated citizens places the individual in the flock of those who cultivate "stupid incredulity". It is worth repeating the concept, because it is of great importance in these times when we are harassed at all times on the net by "cloudy water fishermen", as we used to say in the 20th century.

The way to be free of conspiracy "theories" and false news is to provide ourselves with correct information, always being on our guard. We must always be unbelievers about these boastful unbelievers. Do they know more Cosmology than Einstein? Do they know more cosmonautics than NASA technicians? Do they know more Probability than John Nash? Do they know more Psychology than Steven Pinker? Do they know more economics than Janet Yellen? Do they know more logic than Newton da Costa? Do they know more medicine than Dr. Kenneth Matsumura? They don't know anything worthwhile! They live in darkness and have fun spreading around that we are the wrong ones.

Videos. Was it easy to record video in the 20th century?

At the time of the tapes, which were 16mm, super 8 and a few other formats, recording and editing a short film, video from 1 to 30 minutes, was art restricted to very few people. Norman

McLaren's works were the reference for those who had a camera and wanted to make their short films. They were cultural items, as well as the feature-length films (more than 70 minutes, medium-length tapes being those that have more than 30 and less than 70).

With the arrival of digital videos and the entry on the YouTube platform, art videos continued to exist, mainly in music, but started to live together with informative and pseudo-informative works. Among the latter are those of conspiracy "theories". They are videos based on awkward guesses, in spite of all the creativity that often accompany them, but they are the minority today in the set of erroneous information videos.

Most of the short videos with incorrect information are in the category of false news or mere distortions or denials of scientific or historical facts.

One danger that the unwary are subjected to on the network is that of posts that are out of context, or outdated. They are part of the most innocent harm. Take the case of someone, with credibility in the matter, who recorded a message shortly before the 2014 World Cup stating that the best team was the host, that is, that of Brazil. The speech circulated through the networks and after the great defeat for the Germany team, which won 7 to 1, the post continued to reverberate, as if it were hot news. Now, that football analyst lost the aura he had as a great evaluator of the teams' skills. If the video did not come back through something new, the reputation of the author would suffer no scratch, because everyone knows that "mining and election, only after verification", as politician Magalhaes Pinto taught, and this is also true for soccer.

Advisors. Should simple people trust the Internet?

The great behavioral change brought by the short videos on the Internet is that the uninformed, those lacking the minimum training to debate administration, science and art, imagine themselves on equal terms with the professors in the area. A medical professor launches a message with some important recommendation for health prevention and some fool thinks he understood everything the professor said, and then launches a video rebutting that speech. If the petulant had to get to that information by watching an entire feature film, or by reading a text of some ten pages, he would never come to a conclusion, and would not be able to launch his contest post. But the information he gets from the short video gives him that illusory authority.

Thus, in electoral campaigns, the guidance of wise people, a tradition that dates back to Lycurgus, in the 8th century BC, became dispensable by the great mass. It decided to follow the advice of the video launchers, whether they are highly uninformed or medium trained. The most specialized, these are despised, because they speak a language that, even giving the impression of comprehensible to all, has a sophisticated and difficult appearance. The speeches of semi-illiterates take on a much easier world. In the Brexit referendum campaign, the British separation project from the European Union, a leader of a dwarf party spread on a social network that the government's money destined for Brussels would now be used in the island's health system. The argument was fundamental to the final result. He was a liar, and the chief resigned from his post, to plunge into the natural obscurity of his stature, when he began to be questioned.

Flatearthist. How do you explain the belief in the flat Earth?

What happened to the apparent increase in the number of flatearthists in the world is something simple to understand: the Internet facilitates the aggregation of tribes. If before there was a flatearthist in Lisbon, another one in Madrid, another one in Rio de Janeiro and another one in Miami, through social networks they can come together, forming a club. Then they go on tracking the profiles and gathering more supporters of the cause. Reinforced by a number that is, in fact, large, they build up the courage to flaunt their opinion.

There are at least three explanations for flatearthism.

One of them, perhaps the most decisive, is the abundance of *Homo localis*, as opposed to *Homo universalis*. A Homo localis (local man) can be someone open to the world, but with a concern very focused on the place where he lives and the culture of his region. But he can also be someone who does not conceive life outside his small community. For such a man, located for example in northeastern South America, receiving the information that Japan is on the opposite side of the Earth does not make any sense. Your world is the limit of the horizon. If he walks a few more kilometers, for him the horizon remains at the same point. It is easy for him to believe that the Earth is flat. And it is very difficult to absorb the sphericity information. The phenomenon there may occur due to the absence of constructive learning that allows reaching the universality stage.

The second explanation is close to the first and refers to the average educated citizen, but who, even so, continues to be reluctant to accept sphericity. It is the difficulty, or even the inability, that many people have to assimilate the notion of Galilean relativity. If we travel on a road, inside a bus, and beside us we look at another bus, at the same speed, without seeing anything else in the vicinity, we have the impression that the vehicle next to it is stopped. If we quickly look at a tree on the road, on the other side, we will again notice the speed of the bus. So, in relation to the next bus, we are stopped. Regarding the tree, we are 80 kilometers per hour, if this is the speed of the bus on the road.

Thus, from an absolute point of view, the flatearthist is right in three of his "findings":
- The ocean is flat
- The Earth is immovable
- The Sun revolves around the Earth

From a more general point of view, which is the relativistic one, he lives a great illusion. The ocean seems flat to an observer sitting on the beach, up to a distance of 3.5 kilometers. But from there, a boat that distances from us begins to disappear on the horizon. And we know that the boat did not slip at the edge of the Earth because it could be back in a few hours. And because of this ability to see beyond the horizon, we accept the notion that the Earth is not immovable and that it revolves around the Sun.

The third explanation, which does not exclude the previous two, is that the flatearthist may be a victim of Asperger's Syndrome, a mental problem whose carrier, among other disorders, does not interpret connotation in linguistic signs, but only denotation. As a child he learns at school that the earth is a sphere, however, slightly flattened at the poles. This information creates a clash in the learner's understanding. Is it flat or is it spherical? That it is spherical, it is not very visible to the child, but that it is flat is what appears before our eyes. Having to choose one of the two situations, something that does not concern a child who does not have the disorder, he tends to stay with the easiest, discarding the possibility of sphericity. In the English language, this group believes in flat Earth, not planed Earth.

There is also a suspicion that the non-acceptance of Galilean relativity may be one of the limitations of people with Asperger's Syndrome, along with the rejection of connotation, the passion for following orders (sometimes even stupid) and verbal incontinence. The non-relativity may be the reason for the rejection of the connotation.

Many flatearthists continue their regular studies, and reach a level of education that allows them to develop arguments for the cause, always in open disagreement with the scientific results. Let us look at a small glossary of the concepts defended by them.

Artist. Fun professional who lives by dilapidating the public purse and spreading lies, such as anthropogenic global warming and heliocentrism.

Copernicus. A crazy priest who, in his senile age, wrote that the Earth revolves around the Sun.

Correct. Core of the expression "politically correct", which is the citizen's way of being politically wrong.

Einstein. A mad scientist who tried to correct Newton, but wrote a theory that he himself did not understand.

Flatearthism. Photographs showing the sphericity of the Earth are simple manipulations, since the Earth, discounting mountains and valleys, is entirely flat.

Geocentrism. The valid theory about the position of the Earth, but that has been dismissed by scientists who like to complicate things.

Globalism. Attempt to impose a universal religion contrary to the Judeo-Christian tradition.

Internet. A space of communication that is the result of divine inspiration, not of modern science, which is all wrong.

Nationalism. Rejection of globalism, with exemplary overwhelming in Brexit, glorious moment of the British Conservative Party.

Newton. Author of a dysfunctional law (ones said to be from Galileo) called "Principle of Inertia".

Nicotine. A lawful substance that makes flatearthists happy, and although scientists say otherwise, it does not cause pulmonary emphysema or any other disease.

UN. A collusion of nations proposed by Einstein in 1945, to implant the "globalism".

Teacher. Teaching professional who needs to be controlled in order not to teach children the aberrations that scientists try to impose.

Reporter. Press professional specialized in the production of "fake news".

Satellite. Artificial satellite is a big lie from NASA, to justify Newton's wrong theories.

Warming. Core of the expression "global warming", which is a madness of leftists.

Divinity. How do flatearthists explain the Internet?

The explanation for the functioning of the Internet, as a divine work, is not publicly admitted by any flatearthist, but it is the only one that fits in his profession of faith.

Because the computer, including the class of smartphones, is a device that contains the accumulation of all the science developed since the times of Thales of Miletus to the conceptions of Zuse, Lilienfeld, Bardeen, Shannon, Turing and von Neumann, passing by almost all great physicists in history, as well as other mathematicians such as Pascal and Leibniz.

Each time we call an action to be processed on the screen - or further processed internally, such as sending text to the printer, or message via an audio - the result we obtain is only possible through a mathematical function, or a mathematical process known as algorithm. And what appears on the screen is not done with chalk, wax or ink, but with electrons.

Stationary satellites, which receive and retransmit Internet signals, are in space by equations left by Newton for this purpose, and which are equations of the Universal Theory of Gravitation, developed by him. Gravitation implies sphericity and rotation. Asteroids are not spherical, because their mass is small, compared to that of planets and stars, and therefore has little force of attraction to attract other bodies, which would lead to the approximate spherical shape.

[According to Newton's theory, the gravitational force F between two bodies **a** and **b** is calculated as $G*m_a*m_b/r^2$, therefore dependent on the mass of both and the distance **r** between them (G, a value well below one billionth, represents the universal gravitational constant). Using the formulas of gravitational force and centripetal force (m*v²/r), Newton deduced the escape velocity formula, which accounts for a square root of 2G*m/r. It is with these calculations that aerospace technicians "hold" satellites in the sky. Without gravitation, any artificial satellite launched into space would immediately fall.]

Isaac Newton: Satellite orbits

As there is no other alternative in the scientific world to explain the functioning of the Internet, the fact that flatearthists disown all this implies the implicit acceptance that it is the product of an alleged divine magic, a magic that is far beyond the understanding of the most important clerics. of the most sensible religions on the planet. Clerics, like all sane people, understand the Internet through their scientific foundations.

Manipulation. How are rubbishes scattered?

Trying to sell their stupid disbelief as if it were skepticism, flatearthists and other deniers can sometimes trick you. But those who are already wary of them do not waste time looking or listening to their bullshit. However, if the post is circulating intensely, if it "went viral", it is because it is somehow convincing, in addition to using the manipulation tactics that are already highly recognizable.

Videos that are accompanied by advertising that "TV censored" and "it has already been removed from YouTube", with the request "forward without mercy", these already say what they came for. These are news that, admittedly, circulate through the underground of journalism. Most of the time it is an obsolete subject, as the speeches demanding "the end of the 14th and 15th annual salaries of the congressists".

What the incautious does not know is that in societies whose governments do not adopt official censorship of the press, the news that is not printed in the newspapers or does not appear on radio and TV programs is only one that is irrelevant and lying. When true news is relevant and the head of the newsroom, or the owner of the news outlet, does not like it, it goes to the footer, without the right to any prominence.

Competition. What makes the press avoid lies?

One of the controls for this practice is competition. If the New York Times had not published the note on the discovery of chemical weapons deposits in Iraq, which was done reluctantly and without any fanfare, a competitor would have brought the information to light, and with force, in order to shake off the credibility of the New York newspaper, which for years maintained the non-existence of those weapons.

If in a given country, the press works as a monopoly, so there is no reliable information, although all news is given without objection. But if the journalistic production is subject to a competitive system, to a healthy competition model, the pretentiously citizen journalism of the Internet video producers can only be in the category of focus on fake news.

This obscurantist world of manipulators cannot be confused with an alternative professional press, as is the case with the virtual newspaper Mediapart, a group of French reporters highly experienced in the work of the traditional press. Every major country has its Mediapart emulators, and we need to give them credit. They are serious journalists and are engaged in the task of verifying the veracity of the information.

Verification. How can we separate the wheat from the chaff?

An important test against the producers of fake news videos is the verification of their writing ability. Speaking, everyone speaks. To write, in journalism, it is necessary to undergo some training. Counterfeiters also make written posts, and even use Tweet, but their written messages are provocations, often in the form of questions, not informative texts. Journalists know how to produce opinionated texts and informative texts, without allowing contamination of one into another. The producers of fake news do not have this ability, and they demonstrate this lack when they try to produce written messages.

In posts that are forwarded on social networks, the first step to be taken by the receiver of the message is to check the origin. If it is news from a major newspaper, whose web address is at the bottom of the post, one can rely on seriousness, because hardly a false newscaster reaches the sophistication of manipulating the source. The nonsense that we see passed on by our naive friends comes from crude portals, never from major news organizations.

Knowing the world of science, knowing the world of administration, having information about the communication companies, these are all mechanisms for preventing virtual falsehoods.

It can be argued that most do not have this training, and therefore are susceptible to bait in the hands of the scoundrels. This is a fact, and it is the biggest reason why less informed people need to be alerted about the dangers that lie ahead of them. Swallowing strange news at face value is very reckless. When in doubt, the citizen can always consult someone more well-read. It has always been like this in the history of the world, and this reality does not change with the widespread access to smartphones. The opposite is the case.

Scientific. How do scientists organize tests?

Scientific work is questioned by semi-literates as if they have the authority to do so, and with that they get a large audience, because their speech is easier to absorb than that of scholars. For example, forming control groups to study new drugs, or to apply existing drugs in use against new diseases, has been an attitude practiced for centuries by pharmacologists, biochemists, biologists and doctors. Taking individuals affected by the disease being researched, a group A, say, 100 people, is undergoing treatment with the drug in question, while another group of the same size, the B group, receives care to placebos base. If the medicine is really promising, group A will be cured, while in group B only those moved by a lot of faith, and who trusted in the efficacy of the product they ingested, without knowing it was a placebo, will be free of the disease. If in group A the proportion of cured people is significantly higher, the efficacy of the remedy will be attested, as long as the fact is replicated in several other research centers, to avoid interference from some undetected local factor.

Control groups are made up of people who sign the consent to participate in the process. If the situation of these people is that of terminally ill patients, with a few days to live according to the medical evaluation, they will only gain by accepting to participate in these tests.

Then a new problem arises when the flatearthists divulge the name of a medicine that is being researched and initiate campaign so that all the patients receive the treatment. The academy may even give in to pressure, but if the medication causes, instead of a cure, harmful side effects in patients, those meddling flatearthists will not be put as responsible for the disaster.

Of course, scientific methods are not infallible, but possible procedural flaws must be analyzed and repaired by those who know the subject. Otherwise, we have the situation of that naughty individual who never entered an aircraft and the first time he enters an aircraft he wants to explain the control panel to the pilot.

Failures. What mistakes can a news reporter make?

The need that we have today to oppose the work of professional journalists to the irresponsible use of social networks in the dissemination of news and lies should not hide the fact that the press professionals also make mistakes, at one time or another, as well as doctors in their surgeries are also at risk of making mistakes. It is not because of the sporadic error of the doctor that the citizen will come to trust the charlatans. The mainstream press also makes its mistakes, and we must all be vigilant about this.

There are at least three possible types of gaps or mistakes in the daily work of news professionals. They come from circumstances that have behind:

- The reporter who makes up facts
- The reporter who errs by ignorance
- The reporter who practices "supressio veris"

The role of the reporter who makes up facts is unusual, but there is at least one scandalous case. Years ago, a leading New York Times professional, who had achieved renown for his seemingly serious work, was spotted making up news. Obviously, he was fired and unmasked. This case is an exception in the work of the many thousands of journalists around the world, fulfilling their task with precision.

The second case, of the reporter who errs by ignorance, is more common and less reprehensible, because the biggest blame lies with the education system. In the early 1980s, an article written in an important newspaper, now extinct, brought the statement that the X-ray machine had the ability to make the human body transparent, allowing bones to be seen through skin and flesh. Now, there is no transparency! What the device does is launch a discharge of electrons, which engraves a plate, hitting the points under some more solid bulkhead, which in this case are the bones, with less intensity. Still in the communications field, agency advertisers made announcements at the beginning of the 21st century about the launch of a major radio station. They coined a phrase that, for connoisseurs of basic science, belittled the new vehicle. The phrase was: "The news at the speed of sound". Now, the radio transmits at a much greater speed than that of sound. The radio wave is electromagnetic, just like the light wave. Its approximate speed is 300 million meters per second, while the speed of sound, which is transmitted in a purely mechanical wave, is 343 m/s, therefore less than half a kilometer per second. A news broadcast in Tokyo would take many weeks to reach Rio de Janeiro if it came at the speed of sound.

The practice of "supressio veris", the suppression of the truth in fact, almost never constitutes a defect on the part of the reporter or his employer. A notable example is that of the photos of the many killed in the collapse of the Twin Towers by the Bin Laden pilots on September 11, 2001. It was a consensus among major media outlets in the United States that the photos showing the fallen and broken bodies would not be published. It was a healthy decision, because in general it is the morbid merchants of tragic news that exploit this type of image.

Often the reporter finds himself in a moral obligation to hide certain facts in the reports he writes because he is aware that revealing them can result in huge economic losses, deaths or even wars. For example, an ecological disaster of Dantesque proportions was caused in the Atlantic Ocean some time ago. The perpetrator of the crime was easily traceable, but technicians and the press decided to stop the investigation, after disclosing some improbable clues as a means of deviating the focus to diversionary speculations. Pointing out the criminal would ignite the warrior spirit on the part of the on-duty authority, as was already known. Another demented war was averted, almost certainly.

Dogmatism. Are scientific results infallible?

The journalist must always be alert not to become antipode to the flatearthists, in the sense of starting to cultivate blind faith in the scientific results embraced by the academy in his time. Let us imagine the moral situation of the reporter who closed ranks with eighteenth-century doctors adept at the method of bleeding as the last word in cures. Doctors were trained to believe it, but media professionals were free to join or not join that insane cause. It would be enough to think a little more deeply to realize that the best policy was to avoid affixing your signature to the approval of that practice.

Science is supported by evidence and tests. The instruments that today seem safe and efficient to guarantee the validity of certain theses, these can be improved tomorrow, and can even be made obsolete as a result of new discoveries. Before the work on fermentation carried out by Louis Pasteur in the middle of the 19th century, it was legitimate to dream together with Aristotle about the phenomenon of spontaneous generation. Can life arise from purely inorganic materials? Can it rise from the ashes? We didn't know. Aristotle's suspicion remained a hypothesis to be considered. Pasteur was in the current that thought that idea was not serious. And he showed, with his boils and fermentations, that the substances that shelter the life of microorganisms can be easily sterilized, without any spontaneous generation occurring there after.

Decades before Pasteur, a valid principle in his area, Chemistry, was the existence of the phlogiston. It was an invisible element, something like the force of gravity, responsible for fueling combustion. But Antoine de Lavoisier demonstrated, before being guillotined for fiscal and political issues, that the element that nourishes combustion is oxygen. The phlogiston left the scene.

At the beginning of the 20th century, Albert Einstein validated and divulged the result of the experiment that overthrew another very old belief, which was the one that postulated the existence of ether, also an invisible substance that, presumably, constituted the universal bed upon which the celestial stars sail. Analyzing the famous experiment by Michelson and Morley, made in 1987, of sending a ray of light to the Moon and observing its reflection on Earth, Einstein fully agreed with the interpretation that the result obtained was only possible if the ether were discarded.

Currently, these fragile principles are practically removed from Physics and Chemistry, but in the fields of Biology and Psychology the academy still walks on mobile bridges. It is always prudent to escape from adopting as a dogma any principle that is contested within the research centers themselves.

This concerns, certainly, people who deal with professional journalism, education and research. Because the followers of flatearthists on social networks have their own certainties. One of the new phenomena is that of relatives trying to impose on the doctor that he give the patient medicines that are still in the testing phase, with no conclusion about efficacy and dangers in side effects, just because some crazy people have spread over the Internet that this medicine represents salvation. As there are many deaths due to this hasty application of the medication, the correct attitude of the doctor is to prepare a document in which the patient and bossy relatives sign their responsibility for the intervention. If the doctor gives in only by oral insistence, without a subscription, he may face major problems in the event of death.

Convincing. Is it easy to indoctrinate someone over the Internet?

Although the belief in the potential of digital media as a convincing tool is widespread, this turns out to be an erroneous opinion. When you advertise your adherence to a given cause through social networks, you can form a club, bringing together many supporters of the same idea. Anyone who sees it from the outside imagines that you are convincing all those people. It's a mistake. What happens, as in the case of flatearthists, is the group identification. If I am an admirer of Gabriel Fauré's musical work and I try to form a page dedicated to him, soon I can get thousands of followers, but they are citizens already fond of that type of work, even if they have not paid much attention to that composer before.

If the Internet user is anti-liberal and forms a club for cultivators of that political line, he will add those already converted. A liberal who tries to join the group, by courtesy, will only reinforce his previous position as a liberal. Likewise, a liberal who creates a page to join liberals, he will not be able to convert anti-liberals to his cause, if the doctrinal work is done virtually. If you are a Buddhist and want to take a Catholic to your flock, or vice versa, you must do it analogically, by telephone or by personal conversation, even by handwritten letters.

However good your arguments may be, do not convince the other if your communication vehicle is digital. It is difficult to accept this fact because many distorted political campaigns on the Internet work. But we have to agree that if we alarm people with a lie and, from that, they vote for what we want, we are working with information asymmetry, not with doctrinal content. The lie about the health budget in the Brexit campaign paid off because the British believed that specific information. If it is exhaustively disclosed that a given candidate will distribute, after being elected, 500 grams of gold to each working citizen, that candidate for the post will win the election, as long as the information seems credible to the vast majority of voters (certainly the conversation would not progress within the electorate) well prepared from Switzerland, which is an exception). Political analysts understood that the comfortable election of Boris Johnson at the end of 2019 to complete the process of separating from the European Union was proof that voters really wanted Brexit and in that election of the prime minister they only confirmed the decision. It is hasty and flawed interpretation. Reason? The premier was already in office, with his name already established as a leader. This is what gave him the victory, which is explained by the concept of "contradiction of democracy", by Karl Mannheim (once raised to the post, the politician no longer competes on equal terms, because he becomes different). For in the referendum, three years earlier, Brexit won with a very small margin, and guaranteed by voters living in regions far from major centers, and still with great opposition from Scotland. Around London, and in the capital itself, Brexit lost with a big difference. As in almost all plebiscites, the victory belonged to the information asymmetry.

Resistance to adhere to doctrines received through the Internet is an important citizen defense mechanism. It is not something to regret, quite the contrary. This does not mean that people are safe on these virtual browsers. The ease of falling for lies is proof that the most uninformed are at a stage where they put the whole society at risk.

This realization of the impossibility of convincing someone over the Internet of the truth of evident concepts also serves as a warning to those who imagine changing the basic education model, underestimating the value of the face-to-face action of teachers and managers. Education, since Pythagoras, works as a network of bodily relationships. The teacher's iris, the teacher's lips, the warmth of his presence in the classroom, the modulation of his voice, the emotional interaction with the class, all these are indispensable to connect today's student to the sages of Ancient Greece. When we teach Plato's five polyhedra, making drawings on the blackboard, we bring Plato's presence, along with ours, to the classroom. Maria Montessori's proposal to remove the teacher from the classroom, replacing him with a book, notebook and concrete material, is very clever, but clashes with that little visible but effective phenomenon. Even though in the elementary cycle, which is the first three-year period, we decided to apply the idea of the "class without a teacher", Music and Drawing instructors, training subjects, cannot be out (the first must include songs in a foreign language in his repertoire, while the second teaches how to draw the letters of the alphabet, lowercase and uppercase, so that they supply all the deficiencies of classroom teaching work). At higher levels, Khan Academy Internet classes are important, but only as a complement and reinforcement, because nothing can replace the presence of the teacher in junior high and high school classes.

Panning. Are there usable videos made by popular people?

As we have already seen above, not everything is wasteful and not everything is harmful in the universe of the Internet short videos produced by the great mass of network users. Almost all of what is worth seeing is in the categories of music and humor, but here and there some informative video that contains truths and is useful exist. Many unusual situations occur where no reporter has been, or in places where the presence of a press professional happens after the fact to be reported occurs. In these moments the reporter tries to obtain information by listening to those who followed the events. If an ordinary citizen recorded a video at that time, he can present it on the Internet as a contribution to the story. If it is a very relevant event, he can sell the video to some TV channel, because the media are not prejudiced against amateur reporters who act seriously, but, rather, against idlers who are dedicated to spreading false news and promoting intrigue.

Amidst the tangle of short videos on the network, therefore, there is usable material. Precious stones can be found in the middle of the gravel.

Machine. Does machine ownership guarantee power?

Owning a production machine, economist David Ricardo found in the early 19th century, gives its owner immeasurable power. While a camcorder was a very expensive production item, due to the small scale, the cost of its components and also the training required by those who manipulated it, those who made videos, in short, medium or feature film, were very few, and when working under contract, as in the case of those who worked for TV, they were very well paid.

Then digital cameras came on the scene. The first one was created in 1975, at Kodak, by engineer Steven Sasson. It was very large, weighing 8 kilos, and photographed only in black and white. Without the advantage of portability, this creation by Kodak remained in the warehouse. But in 1988 Fuji presented a small camera, the Fuji DS-1P, with a Static RAM memory card, created in partnership with Toshiba. In that year, the Jpeg and Mpeg photo and video standards were launched. Fuji's product, however, did not go to market. The commercialization took place in 1990, with the Dycam machine, launched in the United States. It cost 600 dollars and photographed only in black and white. Very few people bought this camera.

In 1991 Kodak offered the DCS 100 for sale, with a design based on the Nikon F3. DCS was the short for Digital Camera System. From then on, digital cameras began to gain market share. In 1993 the Fuji DS-200F appeared in Japan, with a memory card that later became known as flash memory. After that Fuji machine, Apple QuickTake (1994), Sony Mavica (1997), the Kyocera VP-210 cell phone camera (1999), Olympus E-10 (2000), Creative PC-Cam (2001) and Casio Exilim (2002) came, among many others.

With the popularization of the smartphone, photo and video cameras have become accessible to everyone. That power that the machine gave a few was divided to billions of people, in a very diluted way, and these new owners no longer have the power to control what the camera gave a few in the old days. Many, however, have found that they have great power to disrupt. If you are a well-known artist and you are walking on Avenida Atlantica, in Rio de Janeiro, a slight neglect in which you put a finger in your nostril can be captured on video by a wanderer, who will make an Internet scandal.

With these communication facilities, the flatearthists started to form their clubs, tracking and aggregating pairs around the world, through social networks.

Alarmism. Does easy access to news increase fear?

One of the effects amplified by the popularization of cameras and Internet access is the alarmism that accompanies epidemics and other dangers that carry the possibility of reaching crowds. When the SARS (Severe Acute Respiratory Syndrome) virus, or SARS-Cov (SARS-Coronavirus), identified in China at the end of the previous year, spread around the world in 2003, people received the news at night, on TV, or read it in the morning on printed newspapers. The death rate was 9.5%, a very high number. But the rarefaction in the transmission of the reports, through the traditional news channels, allowed the populations to forget the terrible phenomenon throughout the day and to keep busy in their routine work. Those who dealt with computers throughout the day received reports at any time, but the number of these citizens and their cultural level represented a control in the use of news as a weapon of dissemination of despair.

In 2020, the migration of the coronavirus (SARS-Cov-2), also, apparently, originating in China, brought, on the viruses of previous epidemics, the difference in the speed of infection which is very high. Covid-19, a disease caused by the new coronavirus, has a worldwide average lethality rate of 4.7%, although in Italy it has exceeded 11%. With initial symptoms manifested in cough, fever and sore throat, the disease is aggravated when it leads to breathing difficulties, with accumulation of fluid in the lung. The great dread is heightened by the fact that the majority of those infected show no symptoms, acting only as transmitters, and also by the increased lethality in older people. As TV broadcasters fear to be left behind in the race for the audience, they compete with the Internet and hammer out data on the progress of the pandemic every minute.

The severity of covid-19 is undeniable. But the global panic it brought would have been much less if, as in the cases of SARS at the beginning of the century, few people had access to smartphones.

Paradigms. Can Smartphone help with literacy?

What has to be managed as a novelty is not the arrival of information to the great mass, but the widespread possession of machines that previously were used to give power to relatively prepared people and, suddenly, reached the hands of all citizens.

Let nobody consider taking the machines of the popular citizen around the planet, or restricting their sales to them. The benefits of such access are vastly greater than the losses. So what is needed is to guide the populations, and to create new human relationship paradigms.

To name just one of the gains from this new reality, let us think of the case of illiterate adults. While literacy was necessary to access content from documents, books, newspapers and magazines, with TV supplying the hunger for information and entertainment, now with the smartphone no one feels comfortable marching off. Each adult wants to have his own, and to manipulate it it is necessary to be literate.

Furthermore, with all citizens having one of these machines, once respect for science and authority is resumed, it will be much easier than before to train people, bringing them quality information, within their absorption possibilities.

Chapter 5. The end of intuition

Many services that involve communication can be done remotely, but not those that require physical contact, or even an "eye to eye".

Telemedicine. Is Internet Medical Examination effective?

Completing almost a decade of the popularization of smartphones, medical authorities are still discussing whether or not to release telemedicine, given that doctors and patients can interact thousands of kilometers away from each other, without prejudice to the understanding of mutual statements. The whole problem is that, while one sees and listens to the other, they do not feel. Sound and image from one to the other are transformed into binary electronic codes that the machine processes, "understands" and transmits, reproducing the environment in which the data were captured.

This interface, which is electronic coding, discards the content that would exist in face-to-face empathy. The fact that the doctor sees the patient's face, color of clothing and iris on the screen cannot even add to the perception of heat, even if a thermometer is showing a number. Two different people with a temperature measured as 36°C are not strictly with the same temperature.

Other issues are changed in digital communication. The tone of the speaker's voice, with the coding and decoding processed by the communication system, reaches the interlocutor as something slightly similar to the tone of voice emitted, but it will never be equal to the tone perceived in person.

Anamnesis (*ana* = bringing back, *mnesis* = memory, in Greek), which is the doctor's conversation with his patient with the aim of evaluating, through empathy, the general condition of the examinee, is seriously impaired when operated remotely. On a line telephone, analog, something could be used, but not on a smartphone, or on a video conference based on digital processes.

Religiosity. Should clergy do baptisms over the Internet?

In times of epidemics that lead to quarantine, it is important that the faithful receive the word of their religious minister. It is not the case of the atheistic citizen or the agnostic, but for the religious person, depriving him of this interaction is an act of great recklessness. Since physical presence is prevented, virtual communication is valid.

In the case of the Catholic worship, the Mass, the faithful will not have access to the host, as they no longer have when they see the ceremony on TV. Receiving the host and swallowing it represents the Catholic's concrete connection with the early Christians, since the evangelist Saint John, according to the Vatican, instituted the practice, as an answer to Jesus of Nazareth's request for the remembrance of the Last Supper. It is a network of relationships that is two millennia old, and that requires face-to-face action as the basis for its continuity. Transforming the ingestion of the host into a virtual practice would mean not a change in nature, but the end of an institution, which is the Eucharist.

Anything that depends only on the word, without the need for physical contact, can work in religious acts. But ceremonies such as the *bar-mitzvah* (bat-mitzvah, for girls), which corresponds to Catholic Chrism (Confirmation), baptism, marriage, priestly ordination and the anointing of the sick, all of this only makes sense in person.

If the anointing of the sick, in cases of terminally ill patients who are in the last hours of life, cannot wait, and a virtual action can serve to comfort the dying person, other sacraments should not use this subterfuge of urgency. There were religious ministers who performed baptisms over the Internet. The believer who was baptized in this way must know that he participated in an unreasonable act. That's not what the Internet is for.

Contracts. Is it healthy to hire employees virtually?

We begin to address here the great difference between digital and analog in the field of human intuition.

A man of 90 years, a person of possessions, who lived alone, hired a young woman as a caregiver for the elderly. He had his first contact with her for Internet, and he sympathized with her, placing her trust in this phase of virtual interaction. Weeks after being hired, the young woman took companions who ransacked the elderly man's apartment and, most likely because he reacted, or to prevent him from locating them later because he knew they were friends with the caregiver, they committed larceny. The murder, however, if it happened as a precaution on the part of the offenders, did not prevent the police from unraveling the crime.

The destruction of the power of intuition is, therefore, in the first contact.

If you work in the HR (Human Resources) sector of a company and want to attract candidates for a job using the Internet, you should avoid looking at their faces or hearing their voice before face-to-face contact. If ten candidates come up, wait to get to know your face and voice when you schedule the face-to-face meeting in your office. Hence, you use your old analog intuition to decide which candidate fills the profile the company needs. If you have a good background in Administration, you know that height or skin color bias will not interfere either.

Someone will say that even with the care to get to know first in face-to-face, analog mode, intuition can fail. This is an undeniable fact, but what is at stake here is the realization that, even with the risk of failure, intuition used analogically works entirely, while in virtual mode it disappears.

Before we were aware of the fact, delinquents already dominated it. Let us take any among them. Suppose he looked for jobs, in person, even with the mere intention of hitting, like the pretended caregiver of the elderly, once his goal was never to work hard, really. He went around several employers, who did not hire him, because it was enough a first look in the eyes for the near-future boss to see deep down the candidate's weakness of character. So it was with each of the intended employers. After half a dozen unsuccessful attempts, the smart scammer decided to use the smartphone, showing himself to the future employer only in virtual mode. Once the contact was made and "mutual" trust established, the thief introduced himself. And the boss no longer had the power, by his intuition, to assess whether the individual was reliable or not, because he already knew him virtually. Physiognomy, tone of voice, shape of the hairstyle, all this was already familiar, but in a misleading way.

Internet contracting, therefore, in addition to not having the powerful analog intuition, it also submits to the risk of adverse selection: while the honest citizen does not shy away from accepting making a first contact in person, the bandit, tired of being discarded by the analog intuition, seeks to hide in the virtual showcase, which transforms all human beings into brilliant, calm, beautiful, correct and complete people.

Policy. Is the cloud candidate reliable?

At this point the situation is more worrying, because party politics aims to regulate everyone's life. Voting for a candidate who met on the Internet, even if there is later analog contact, can be an exercise in liberty, but not equality and fraternity. If the manager's intuition fails to hire an employee whose first contact was virtual, the voter's intuition is much more vulnerable. With his intuition hampered by virtual illusionism, he puts the lives of all his fellow citizens at risk each time he enters the polling booth and endorses the choice he thinks came from an independent and sovereign decision.

The counting of votes made electronically is excellent, with results determined at the speed of lightning. But if a significant part of the electorate went to the ballot box to vote for a candidate who first appeared to it in virtual mode, the whole modernity of the counting will prove to be fruitless, like a Picasso painting with gouache under torrential rain.

Intuitive. How does intuition develop?

It is very important to emphasize that intuition is not something that springs from nothing, by spontaneous generation. Many think that intuiting is to arrive at a perception through an inspiration coming from the celestial spheres, but this idea is wrong. A child on the day of birth already has some intuition formed by its learning in the months of uterine life, and by its ontological learning, that is, of the species. An adult, likewise, is able to have intuitive perceptions because he previously had experiences, or studies, that gave him the instruments for that. If Pascal sensed the model of the first adding machine, it was because he was already dealing with operations. A professional from a popular music label intuits that a particular song will be successful because he already has the experience of what kind of song wins the audience. Those who do not have this experience will make the guess based on their personal taste, not based on the taste of the consuming public.

So, when we first look into the eyes of a person we have just met and see him as a sincere and honest person, this skill of ours does not come out of the blue. Yes, it does from a Psychology apprenticeship that we practiced since childhood. We scan the faces of our generous and good-natured friends to see if we can find anything in common with them. Likewise, we analyze the face and expression of those who make mistakes and who are weak in character. We cannot describe with words these common traits that exist between these individuals of questionable ethics, but we know that they exist.

In digital photographs, or digital videos, this learning does not take place, because there everyone is beautiful, just, virtuous, generous and wonderful. Of candidates for political office, there is no need to speak.

Plato gave the recipe for preventing these evils 24 centuries earlier. One chooses the candidate who one knows personally, whose first contact is eye to eye. This limits the democratic polis to a maximum of 5,040 citizens (factorial of seven), which is the limit amount for the voter hear the speaker in the agora. How to do with more populous circumscriptions? Now, we use the representative and federative system of modern times. In the case of parliaments, preferably with the proportional vote.

Children. Should a small child have a smartphone?

A much more critical case is that of controlling children's access to the Internet and the use of children's images by relatives. Most parents post photos and videos of children without ever thinking about the risk they are exposing themselves and their children to. But the biggest danger is in allowing young children to access the Internet and even the computer itself, which is often used for electronic games and other hobbies.

It is almost a consensus among psychiatrists that the use of computers or smartphones by children under 30 months of age can seriously impair language development. There is no single pattern for this damage, but an easily observable loss is the delay in the ability to speak. From one moment to the next, at the beginning of the 21st century, children began to start the process of intelligible speech from the age of two, no longer from one-year-old as it was before.

This one year delay in starting interaction with others through speech at the most important stage of learning acquisition certainly brings gaps in the child's mental development.

Professor Valdemar Setzer, one of the founders of the Computer course at the University of Sao Paulo (USP), began in the 1970s to alert parents and teachers in publications and lectures on the dangers of exposing children to the computer screen. The computer, although it is a silly machine, which does exactly what it is told to do, requires, for its handling, a certain maturity in dealing with Logic. As the child does not have this outlined yet, the machine will force an early intellectualization, which, according to the professor, makes the child skip stages in its psychic development, in an unhealthy way. The child's frequent interaction with a fool machine can cause the child to grow up as a fool person.

If children's use of a disconnected computer (offline) is already questioned, due to the damage it can cause, allowing them to use it online is highly reckless. Bill Gates, who became a millionaire producing and selling software, had a requirement when his children were young: They will only use the computer when they know enough English and a lot of Mathematics. It is the word of those who know the danger.

Analog. Is it wise to give up the analog world?

Analog mode is a culture of several millennia and it persists within the digital world, sometimes as a format only, sometimes as a core. With the spread of digital watches, many children grow up without learning to read the time on a hand watch. It turns out that many tower clocks, even with a digital machine, have an analog dial, sometimes even with the time in Roman numerals, following tradition.

Reading the time in digital format is not something you need to learn, because you only need to know how to read Indo-Arabic numerals. But the child does not learn alone, except for one or another gifted, to interpret the hours on the hand clock, that invention by Ctesibius of Alexandria (285 B.C., 222 B.C.) that still has a trajectory of centuries, most likely. This is what teachers or parents need to teach.

A friend of this present author, an aircraft pilot, who works in the State of Florida, has the habit of using a small passbook when he is in the cabin, in mid-flight. Whenever there is a new maneuver indicated on the panel, he checks that passbook, sometimes scribbling in pencil to check the results. If one day the machine is out of order and it makes a maneuver that will make the plane hit the mountain, he will immediately have checked this breakdown. One or the other, dazzled by technology, may be surprised by this attitude of the pilot, but if prudence is a valuable thing on the ground, at the height of the clouds it must have much greater value.

(It is necessary to distinguish analog that deals with analogy, as in "analogical reasoning", from analog that is opposed to digital - these are very different situations.)

Fault. Are we to blame for fooling children?

When the child is born, its umbilical cord is cut, it sees the mother, it sees those present in the birth room, it cries, all this is analog life for it. There may be a digital device in the room, but that does not concern it. The digital world begins to configure itself for the child as it grows. To immerse it early in digital life or preserve it, to give it access to smartphones and the Internet at the appropriate time, that decision is up to us adults.

Anyone who claims to have given their child early access to the Internet without causing harm should keep in mind that it may be an exception to the statistical rule. You should not want to play with that.

If the child develops a delay in the speech domain, some other failure in the use of language or other mental sequelae due to exposure to electronic screen devices before acquiring maturity, the adults are responsible, because they care of them. There may also have been a congenital problem, but this, in today's world, does not represent the majority of cases, unless there is harmful interference in pregnancy, as was the problem of using thalidomide in the malformation of fetuses, or the most common recent pest of Zika virus.

In the education of the child, there is no doubt that the analog must have priority over the digital. Providing literacy to children with machines and instructing them with digital devices, such as robots, until they reach adulthood and enter university and be owner of themselves, this is a possibility, but, over time, when damage caused by such paternal behavior is mapped, it will be considered a serious crime.

Cursive. Should we abandon handwriting?

Some federative units in the United States decided to abandon cursive letters in literacy processes since 2014. The argument is that the digital world dispenses with this type of handwriting. Now, if it is not taught in the Montessori "sponge" phase (phase of easy absorption of knowledge, when the brain is like a sponge), after growing up the person will not learn to read the handwriting, the old cursive letter. Anyone who is accustomed to writing in Latin characters does not realize this, but the reader can analyze a text in Russian with both types of writing, cursive and press. You can also make the comparison in Greek, but Russian accentuates the difference better. However accustomed the reader may be to Russian press writing, looking at a handwritten letter, in cursive, gives the impression that no Russian letter is known by the reader. It is, therefore, a literacy distinct from that involved in press letters.

In the Spanish language, it is common to use "bastard" letters as a synonym for "cursive" letters, because the common type of letter we use today is a bastardizing of that refined and flowery writing that was used in documents in the Renaissance. This adjective given to the letter is a burden against it, but it should not shake anyone's convictions about the importance of teaching its mastery in childhood. If teaching how to see the time on an analog clock is important, teaching cursive is even more so.

The debate is open between literacy teachers and psychologists, about whether or not to bury cursive in school at once. However, unless this type of letter is used in everyday life, a person who can only write in print will always give the impression of someone who has evaded important learning, someone who has been plundered in his rights. In addition, the debate remains lively because it is not yet known what are the losses in the development of the apprentice caused by the lack of that training.

One of the ways to overcome the dilemma is to teach children to use lowercase italics. They are a middle ground between press writing and cursive writing. The child who is not trained to write cursive letters will not even know how to exercise this writing, but if it learned to read italic letters early, it will read handwritten texts written in cursive without much difficulty.

Abuses. Are the risks of child abuse high?

Still dealing with the child's access to the Internet and returning to the question of the risk to which it is subjected if left freely in front of the digital device, we should pay attention to some blind spots in navigation.

First, leaving a child alone with a connected smartphone is like leaving it alone in the woods, at the mercy of wolves, ticks and snakes. In the Internet jungle, alone at home it will be in the hands of wolves, ticks and virtual snakes.

Second, a child does not learn to whistle if it has not seen someone else doing it. An immense variety of skills that we develop as we grow up occurs because we have someone to imitate. If the child has access to wolves that teach it early sex, it can become a victim of abuse without much difficulty on the part of the predator.

Third, it is enough for the child, moved by curiosity, to type certain keywords in search engines and then immediately enter a world of perdition, if we can call so the "adult" content pages.

Fourth, there is a massive and millionaire illegal trade in virtual sex with the use of images of children, just as in the analog world there is the clandestine trade in heroin and cocaine.

The safest way to prevent children from falling into te mesh of this insane industry is not to allow them to be alone while accessing the world wide web. The most guaranteed thing is not to give them a smartphone, tablet or computer. At most a cell phone just for telephony.

Even on a non-smart cell phone, without Internet, the child has an electronic calculator, which is a negative thing for those who are learning the rudiments of Arithmetic. The most responsible educational experts recommend that children use electronic calculators freely only after they have mastered the multiplication tables and the four operations. Before that, what does not harm the brain is the count made on the pencil.

Education. How should we use the Internet in education?

Those dazzled by technology, who are never the people who develop it, but only those whose relationship with the object is purely for consumption, live dreaming of a world in which all education takes place remotely, or, alternatively, carried out by robots in the classroom. The human element, above the studenthood, remains only in the laboratory, manipulating the machinery.

The defenders of this new world speak and defend these things without talking to those responsible for creating the new machines and the programs that make them usable. These are unanimous in recommending caution. If there are dazzles among them, they are there as consumers, trying to find a place among the creators, but they will never create anything substantial.

Computers and the Internet are splendid tools to support the educational process. At this point in the 21st century, we cannot imagine an education system that misses these resources. It would be a monumental delay in life.

But not everyone knows the right dosage. And, like with any effective medication, exaggeration on the dose becomes poison. At university and high school, until recently teachers used to print material, in many cases using the web, to deliver to students, so they could study and exercise. Nowadays, with widespread access, they don't even need to print, except the tests. Just they give them the virtual address and the students go after them, on their machines. This is very healthy.

Searches on search engines help in ways never dreamed of before. But there are gains in this only if teachers are giving the necessary guidance. Writer Umberto Eco (1932-2016), professor in Milan, made a survey launching random words in the search engines to verify the results. In his account, 2% of what appeared on the screen was usable, relevant. The rest was either bullshit or something unrelated to the typed term.

Umberto Eco: Warning about baloneys

If a student searches, for example, for explanations on a history topic, without being aware of which pages are reliable, he may fall into a disguised Nazi page (explicit Nazi preaching has been banned from the network since the end of the 20th century), or fall into the hands of a deceiver, who thinks to know something about the topic and knows nothing seriously. If you are researching Mathematics, you can be taken to a lesson that presents some writing without rigor of language. And Modern Mathematics without this rigor can seem like anything but Mathematics.

In the face of all these obstacles, taking distance education without proper precautions is an enemy of education. There are situations in which distance learning is convenient and recommended, but these are specific types of learning. A distance higher education course is very valid, in certain fields, but for someone who has already graduated from university. For example, someone who has a degree in Literature, in person, and wants to study History in course at a distance, will not have considerable losses, if he is a person dedicated to studies. The opposite is no longer defensible, once the Latin subject is no longer mandatory in high school. If a citizen trained in another area wants to study

English, for example, he has to go through face-to-face Latin courses at college, and preferably also for initial English language courses.

Even more delicate is the prospect of training someone in medicine in the form of distance learning, without any face-to-face cadaver dissection class or other practical and theoretical questions. It's not even good to dream about it. Likewise, it would be highly reckless to train civil engineers without face-to-face Differential and Integral Calculus and Material Resistance classes. A bachelor's degree in Mathematics without face-to-face courses in Calculus and Algebra is also the result of great irresponsibility. But if someone has a degree in Physics and wants to do a Bachelor's degree in Mathematics, things change. A face-to-face mathematician who wants to take a distance course in Physics is also justified, provided he has undergone laboratory courses, which is customary.

At the other end, machines should never be used to teach children to read and write, but adults, over the age of 18, can learn to read and write through the smartphone, without major problems. There may even be a productivity gain in this, in terms of time. The ideal for him would be face-to-face literacy, but he has already suffered the greatest, irreparable damage, of having grown up without the practice of reading. Literacy using machines is an incomparably lesser evil, and its negative effects can be easily diluted in the face of the gain that is learning to read. His situation is very different from that of the small child.

Class. Should we ban cell phones in the classroom?

In 2019 the French government banned the use of mobile phones in the primary school classroom. In Brazil, we had already taken this step years before in the State of Sao Paulo, in a law approved by the Legislative Assembly and sanctioned by the governor. Then, several other States followed that line.

When it is in the teacher's interest, in which case the students work under his guidance, nothing prevents the class from using the smartphone in class to do some research of immediate need, or seek to satisfy some curiosity. The important point is that the prohibition gives the teacher the authority to prevent dispersion in the classroom because of the use of devices that bring a strange occupation to the development of the content. If a naughty student refuses to stow his cell phone or tablet, the teacher can call the student inspector to collect the machine. This is within his competence.

If the student is free to use his cell phone whenever it wants in class, in addition to the possibility of using inconvenient pages on the Internet, it can use the electronic calculator on the device and deceive the teacher, posing as an expert on the multiplication table without knowing anything about it.

And it's not just the multiplication table. Other numerical tables, the results of which are in scientific calculators, are didactic instruments in their own right. For example, learning to consult and use the table of decimal logarithms represents enormous help in understanding the topic. Many textbooks already dispense it, recommending the student to consult the machine, but if it learns logarithms just using the machine, it will learn little of the subject, and will be able to go to the next grade without knowing what is behind that theory, which refers to the deal with the powers of base 10 (or any other base, if we wish), something that will not be visible without the use of the table.

Thus, also in the learning of Mathematics in high school, not only in elementary school, the smartphone with its calculator more hinders that helps.

In addition to Prof. Valdemar Setzer on the early intellectualization and the temerity to skip important stages of childhood and adolescence, we must also add the impediment to the healthy development of intuition in young people. If everything that requires mental operation, reasoning and memory, the educator delegates to the machine, what it is delivering is his instrument of training as a person.

Interference. What damage does much Internet cause?

Many psychiatrists, psychologists, school administrators and other professionals involved in developing human behavior have pointed out some conduct problems caused or accentuated by the intense use of the Internet, especially on social networks. Among them are:

    1 - Alienation
    2 - End of intimacy
    3 - Network dependency

4 - Depression
5 - Practice of lying
6 - Susceptibility to deception
7 - Involuntary transfer of images
8 - Accidents when walking or driving
9 - Inability to be alone and disconnected
10 - RSI (Repetitive Strain Injury)
11 - Deafness
12 - Anxiety
13 - Obesity

Even in the 20th century, with microcomputers and before having easy access to the Internet, teenagers were already at risk of dependence because of electronic games. In South Korea, there was the case of a teenager who spent three days playing uninterruptedly in front of the computer and had a brain seizure, going to the death.

Psychologists are also concerned with the phenomenon of teenagers who refuse to leave home, trapped in a virtual world in the bedroom, whether using social media or spending time on electronic games. Each of these teenagers may be experiencing a feeling of inferiority, as the others post only an idealized, wonderful way of life on the network, and that young man in the bedroom starts to think that his life is mediocre, compared to what the others present through the Internet.

Faced with all these problems, the BBC of London, in written version, presented a set of recommendations to parents and guardians about attitudes towards adolescents:

A) Prohibit the use of electronic devices at mealtime and at least one hour before bed.

B) Supervise the times of use of the devices, to ensure that this does not interfere with the regular activities of the young person, such as eating, sleeping, doing a lesson and interacting with others.

C) Convince the teenagers to use the Internet for the purpose of learning school content and to launch their own content.

D) Talking regularly with teenagers about what they did on the Internet throughout the day, with whom they talked, what they watched, what they shared.

E) Alert to the fact that Facebook, Twitter, Instagram and other social networks are for people over 13, and even so, with due restrictions.

Plunder. What precautions can the user take?

Also WhatsApp, a mobile messaging platform belonging to Facebook, under many complaints of theft of registrations (accounts), published in the newspapers in April 2020 a set of recommendations for the victims of the problem, and for those who want to be prevented.

To those already affected:

1 - Try to recover the account on the cell phone, opening WhatsApp and entering the cell phone number; wait for the confirmation code and follow the steps on the screen.

2 - If the above procedure does not work, send an email to WhatsApp (*support@whatsapp.com*) with the title "Lost/Stolen: disable my account"; include the phone number with the country code and area code in the message.

3 - The account will be deactivated and the user will have 30 days to reactivate it.

For users in general, regardless of whether they have already been cracked or not, the portal suggested entering the *faq.whatsapp.com* page, for more information, after making the following recommendations:

1 - Never share your WhatsApp activation code.

2 - Enable 2-step verification on your WhatsApp account.

3 - Do not install third-party applications or share personal information at the request of anyone via WhatsApp.

4 - Be mistrustful of company calls if the attendant uses very informal language.

WhatsApp alerts serve certainly also for other platforms and other social networks. The last item, for example, on the language of the interlocutor, can be used in many situations. One of them is that of e-mail virus spreaders: Their grammar is hardly civilized. An attentive user easily perceives misspelled words or syntaxes.

Just as viruses and bacteria do their damage to people who do not have antibodies, the bad persons in the digital universe take advantage of newbies, the naive or inattentive ones. Internet companies provide a great service when they guide the user to surf safely.

Lesion. How to prevent muscle pain?

A major problem for users who exaggerate the time spent in front of the computer, or for those who sit in a non-ergonomic way, is the appearance of RSI, Repetitive Strain Injury.

When the first pains appear and the user is suspicious of this damage, the first step is to change the position of the body. If the pain is in the hand or in the arms, perhaps the error is at the height of these in relation to the keyboard, or, in the case of the hand, the position in relation to the mouse.

Changing the position may simply not be enough. If the pain continues, there are two ways: undergoing surgery or taking medication. Brazil has a natural product that is very accurate in solving the problem: Tea of cat's claw, a plant from the east of the country, whose bundle of branches can be found in medicinal plant stores, herbal pharmacies, or at kiosks that sell this type of medicine in the center of big cities. If the new posture in front of the computer is adequate, just take the tea four days in a row, and the pain evaporates.

Judgments. Does live streaming interfere with judgments?

It can be said, without much doubt, that the new custom of the courts to transmit judgments on TV and the Internet came as a consequence of the widespread access to the smartphone. Until the beginning of the 20th century, people did not carry a TV set in their pocket and the judgments were made without interference from broadcasters. What newspapers and TVs did was send their designers. At the end of the session, the drawings were passed on to the newsrooms, just like the reports. The judgments were therefore analog.

The judges' brains and spirits, as we know, are at the mercy of the events that surround them. It has already been found that decisions made before lunchtime are more favorable to defendants than those made in the afternoon without the judges having gone out to lunch. The conclusion is that the hungry judge is more severe and therefore more dangerous for the defendant.

There are, at least any yet published, no studies on the

interference of live broadcasting in court decisions. But it is sharp.

Concerning interference with human behavior in general, there is the case of a 16-year-old girl who was on the top of a building in the center of Sao Paulo looking at the crowd below and looking for just the "appropriate" moment to launch herself from there, committing suicide.

There was a recent late-afternoon TV program on crimes and misfortunes with a huge audience. With rare exceptions, all policemen and criminals dreamed of appearing on this program. The moment the TV news crew arrived at the scene and turned on the camera for recording, pointing it at the young woman, she jumped, having her death recorded and broadcast that day.

The station owner decided to end that program there. With decades of experience in the television business, he knew of his machine's interference in the girl's tragedy.

How many times does a judge exalt himself more than would be reasonable just because it is being broadcast live? And how much can that interfere with his vote at the end of the session? These are questions that have not yet been answered, but that should not remain in the air for decades to come.

A defendant who goes through a manipulated process, and who has public opinion against him, when he is condemned under popular pressure, has no idea that the result against him was induced by the mass, who watched the trial live. And the judge always will deny that he has been shaken by the public.

How can the court be free of this kind of doubt, or suspicion? Returning to the analog pattern, with judgments drawn, no smartphone in the room.

First of all, because it is a morbid interest of the court to find it convenient for judges to show their figures to the general public, even to the miscreants, inducing members of the gang to be convicted. There is no grace, except for the unwary and those dazzled by technology.

Authorities must be preserved from the fury of the brainless, and judges are the first to deserve this deference. In 1960, a Geography textbook recorded that Brazil, with 72 million inhabitants, had 1,000 TV sets. At that time, a judge could show his face at will on TV, because the chance of one of his convicts, or of his partner, being in front of the device at that moment was insignificant. In the 21st century the environment is completely different.

If out of 100 million adults seeing the judge's face at the trial, four people are highly dangerous and have access to that judge, he is taking an oversized risk, a risk that would be close to zero in analog pen-drawn trials.

Can the computer help with the processes? Obviously, yes. And it should. With computerization, the judicial system gained a spectacular advance. However, transforming the judge during the trials into a TV and smartphone artist throws away all the achievements that computing has brought to the area.

Parliament. What parliamentary activity should be opened?

As in the courts, real-time broadcasts of Parliament's sessions need to be questioned. It is very important that the population knows, daily, what is the work that its parliamentarians do. But accompanying them in the polls to get them to act "with the knife in the neck" is not democratic action. A congressman is not an instrument of direct democracy, but of representative democracy. Therefore, he has the task of studying the matters that are being processed in Parliament and must be free to vote according to the conclusions of his studies. If it is up to the voter to pay the representative to study and, at the time of the decision, compel him to follow the will of that citizen who only imagines to know the subject, then the expense with the parliamentarian's remuneration is useless.

This imposing attitude, of wanting to impose the choice on the parliamentarian, is equivalent to that of the relative who wants to force the doctor to apply a new medicine, not yet tested, because he saw on the social network that that medicine is miraculous.

The voter can claim that the congressman is betraying his confidence when he votes secretly. Yes, but this is a situation similar to that in which the citizen hires an employee to manage his business and he begins to practice pecuniary deviations. The boss must not leave his duties to monitor that employee. The right attitude is to dismiss him and hire an honest assistant. In the case of Parliament, the correct thing is to vote for another, in the following elections, trusting that that is a rotten orange in the middle of the healthy orange grocery store. If the Parliament is completely contaminated, it is for one of two reasons: the electoral rule is completely wrong, or it is correct and the legislators only represent the citizens as they are. In the latter case, the solution is to leave the country.

There are no major problems when ordinary votes, for example, on bills, are opened. In general, voters have their smartphones on at other attractions. But when it comes to electing or punishing someone for Parliament, then soap operas, football matches and all other hobbies are exchanged in favor of following that vote. It is at these times that the mafia is awake. A gangster who has worked to elect a representative and sees that he voted against the interest of his criminal organization may have that congressman at gunpoint at the next opportunity.

If the votes, to elect or punish, are closed, their transmissions online, that is, in real time, lose their grace. The result can be reported as news at the end of the count, and that is what will be of interest.

In the name of transparency, many want all voting to be open, but in this way the voter is working against democracy, which, outside the condominium or block, means representative democracy.

Witness. Should testimonials be transmitted online?

A notorious case in Parliament, near the beginning of the 2010s, was the testimony of the wife of a businessman investigated as a corruptor, later sentenced, in fact, to a sentence of decades. With her husband in prison, the couple later divorced, but at the time of the testimony, this outcome could not be predicted.

At the PCI (Parliamentary Commission of Inquiry) that convened her, the tone was that she was an accomplice to her husband's hoaxes.

It was not possible to confirm the accusation to her, but the fact is that the testimony lasted all afternoon, and most of the time she spent crying, in front of the cameras.

That exhibition, on TV and Internet, was a punishment without legal judgment. The Congress received suggestions to avoid repeating this type of show and from there the deponents were spared from these live broadcasts.

A similar problem may arise in witness testimony in court. The witness is there to help clarify the case. Treating it as a criminal, exposing it in live broadcasts for possible public execration is naively perverse.

Netizens. Is the Internet user prepared to interact?

Since the beginning of commercial radio and TV broadcasts in the 1920s, citizens have dreamed of an interactive process, with a permanent dialogue between sender and receiver, not just a business monologue, as it seemed to be the case. Over time, the participation of the listener through the telephone increased, but this was another means of communication, not the Hertzian waves that carry radio and television content. The dream of interactivity came true only with the Internet. In it, the operator of a portal, or of a channel, interacts at any time with the receiver, the Internet user, who is also a sender.

When the Parliament, or the court, broadcasts its sessions live, it must remember that in the new times there is on the other side not a passive spectator, but an Internet user.

There would be no danger, nor would there be any major changes, if Internet users in general were responsible and prepared to deal with the tool they now have in their hands. In such a world we would not have false news, virtual insults, "cancellations" (destruction of reputations), attitudes against scientific methods, false videos (deepfake), grotesque attacks on journalists, virtual manipulation of election campaigns, and so on.

If all these problems exist, it is because the Internet user, as a category, is not to be trusted, at least for now. In all professions, in all activities, there are bad elements, as exceptions. So we have bad doctors, bad lawyers, bad deputies, bad drivers and bad football coaches out there. These do not have much facilitated space in society, because the news spreads, denouncing them. But in the case of the Internet, bad netizens are much more than an exception. And the ones that do the most damage are the ones that hide in pseudonyms.

Attacks. Are serious pseudonyms acceptable?

Philosopher Schoppenhauer was terrified of two types of writers: the one who filled paper ("sausage filler") and the one who wrote under a pseudonym. The one who fills paper has no gift or training for writing, but insists on writing, deceiving the unwary. What he writes under a pseudonym is bad character, according to the philosopher.

Among netizens, the legion of those who use pseudonyms grows like bacteria in culture, because newbies are entering the current without any idea that this is something harmful by nature. Just as the flatearthists discover each other on the net and form their clubs, the users of bad character are joining and adding new unwary, who are forged within their doctrine of bullying.

When the wag uses a playful or unreasonable pseudonym, it provides some key so that the person affected suffers less damage. If an netizen with a pseudonym "Pickaxe" calls you a liar, that no longer gives you much concern, because the offender said what he came from, using a name without seriousness. But if the attacker is called Joseph Brown and uses the pseudonym Andrews Maurice Senna, for example, the result is very different. You have no way of finding out that Andrews is using a false name, and the other users will think it is a real name, someone who attacks you using his real identity.

Some experienced journalists post their stories on blogs and "filter" readers' comments, leaving only minimally polished messages to pass. One of the great news portals in Sao Paulo, after a long period of submission to the world of the badly educated, made the decision to allow responses to be posted only to duly identified subscribers. The disqualified comments simply disappeared.

But social networks, such as Twitter and YouTube, do not provide tools for the selection of comments, except *a posteriori*. Thus we see on Twitter journalists who are attacked daily by arrogant and semi-literate individuals.

Recently, portals like Facebook, YouTube, Twitter and others have started vetoing posts deemed harmful. The downside of the practice is that there is no denying that this is censorship. There is a more appropriate way, which is to record a label on these posts with the inscription "Humor". It is clear that when it comes to humor itself the stripe is not present, so when it appears in some content it is because it is of very low "humor". Internet users stamped in this way would see themselves as the lousy humorists they are. And maybe they would start to get a little social.

Hateful. Do Nazis act out of hatred or fanaticism?
Users who already have a bad character, much petrified, who

are not of the type crowd follower, these will not correct themselves. At most, they will practice some type of abstinence. These are the ones who create the virtual groups that many call "chains of hate".

There is no hatred, because the problem comes from ignorance, bad education and, finally, weakness of character, this one that leads the fool to follow swashbucklers of facade, who live hidden in the den.

The interpretation that Nazi-fascist phalanges are fueled by hatred was presented by Friedrick Hayek in the 1944 book "The road of serfdom". The human flock is regimented by hatred directed at something or someone, and with that one forges the movement that takes the worst to the top.

This is not hate. Writing the work within the outbreak of World War II, without the necessary historical distance, led the author to that view. What occurs is the application of a method. Those who doubt this analysis argue that they lack the intelligence to do so. Intelligence? There is no need for intelligence to put backward programs and make them the ideology of a political party, adding some easy modern theories that do not clash with the rest of the doctrinal body.

The fascism created by Benito Mussolini, former editor of the Avanti newspaper of the Italian Socialist Party, claimed the position of opponent of both liberal democracy and Soviet communism, and embraced a moral attitude towards the capital, separating it into productive capital - desirable - and prey capital - reprehensible. Nazism was formed by adding to Italian fascism some conspiracy theories, the old racism against Jews and blacks, the preaching that usurious international capital was controlled by Jews and the claim to make Germany the center of the world, which should be commanded by the 'pure race' of the 'Aryans'. Hitler, the führer (leader), did not create any of this, but only incorporated the worst anti-democratic ideas that circulated among the Europeans of his time. Warlike cruelty, discrimination against selected enemies, the struggle for perpetual dictatorship, these were all very old.

The novelty of this modern tyranny, which Hitler learned from other equally sick figures, was the policy of exterminating the Jewish people. Until those days, the aim of every general at war was always to defeat the enemy army, dominating its territory and, if possible, commanding or enslaving the defeated. Although Hitler argued, at the end of World War I, that Jews should be expelled from Europe, in position of power, from 1933 onwards, his policy was one of domination. In the early days of World War II, Jews were confined and subjected to forced labor. But since September 1942, Nazism began to put the "final solution" into practice, following a plan drawn up the year before by a man named Reinhard Reydrich, commander of the Central Security Office, when eliminating Jews detained in concentration camps, with the use of gas chamber poisoning.

Doctor Joseph Mengele, who was experimenting with fetuses taken from Jewish women, performing serial forced abortions, said he did not see these women as people, but as objects.

Anyone outside can see hate in this, but they are mistaken. Hatred is an ordinary human feeling, it is not a perversion.

Analytica. How did Cambridge Analytica work?

Likewise, it was not hatred that drove Donald Trump's presidential campaign on the Internet in 2016, as well as other campaigns that followed around the world. Legitimate or not, everything was just a method. If militants here or there cursed, threatened and slandered, all of this is sustained in bad education, put at the service of a cause.

Cambridge Analytica, a British strategic communications company, now extinct, worked for the Trump campaign and was accused of manipulation and dishonesty. For many, it was responsible for the victory of the Republican candidate. However, there is little chance that this is true. It certainly helped a little, like many others, but it didn't go much further.

Its techniques involved collecting citizen data on Facebook and other Internet companies and applying segmentation resources, with "big data" theories (macrodata). Facebook no longer allows strange persons to access user data, but at the time it was possible.

There was nothing new about collecting data and using it commercially. Since the registration of members or users was invented, the practice has been established. Probably, in the Middle Ages, organizers of craft corporations already used the data of their associates to gain some advantage. In the 20th century it was very common for unions to sell, for example, the registration of addresses of members.

In this case of data collected on Facebook or other social networks, the biggest culprits, involuntary ones, were the users, who sent their personal data in a stripped manner, without concern for privacy, modesty and security. These data, which were exposed for free, were in a category close to that of posting images of young children for the world to see.

Voters. Are there measures against false news today?

Again, the use of intuition is impaired, in one way or another, if the voter's source of information is the Internet.

Before, with the indication of friends, of the close authorities, or also of the analog means of communication, the citizen voted with a certain confidence, even if he made a lot of mistakes in his choices. With information about candidates and causes coming only through social networks, those who vote confidently are deluded by the dazzled of technology, because intuition in this environment is just a mirage.

In this sense, Cambridge Analytica was just another instrument, probably one of the least decisive, both in the result of the Brexit referendum in 2016, and in the election of Donald Trump at the end of that year. If there was decisive interference from the Internet in Trump's election (in Brexit it was unquestionable), the weight was diluted among several portals, various social networks and various applications.

Only after the quarantine of March 2020, against the coronavirus, the big digital companies decide to close the siege against the misuse of their channels for spreading lies and campaigns against public health. It is necessary that these companies no longer let their guard down, because neo-Nazis, like all types of criminals, know how to use the Internet well, cloaked in "good" citizens.

Robots. What is the role of virtual robots?

Internet robots, or "bots", have been used since the beginning of the 20th century, already in email services. They are not copper and steel robots, like the old days, but computer programs. The most common use that is made of them is to replicate, in a "viral" way, some content or some message. If a human operator can send 500 copies of a given message over the course of a day, a robot would be able to send 5,000,000 copies of the same post in that time.

The mechanism developed for Internet portals against the invasion of robots was the Captcha (*Completely Automated Public Turing test to tell Computers and Human Apart*). One of the initial models is one that asks the user to fill a given window with a random message generated for the moment. If the user types a character incorrectly, he has a chance to ask the system to generate another two or three sets of symbols, which he will experiment with, until he can activate the desired action. A robot would automatically trigger this action, as long as it doesn't have to enter a Captcha.

For a political party campaign or a commercial product campaign, a robot is a technological marvel. The only problem is the Captcha barrier, or some others that portals will develop.

The robot should not be thought to generate the message. It is created by a human agent. What the bot does is replicate. People who receive it have the impression that the issuer directed the posting to their profile, or to their content recipient. But if the content was sent by a robot, the human issuer has no idea who is receiving it. He knows, yes, the chosen segment. For example, the robot can only target people living in the city of Paris. Or only to users who have already given as personal data that they are older than 60 years.

Algorithms. And how do the algorithms operate?

This choice of segment that the robot makes occurs through an algorithm. The robot itself is a coordinated set of algorithms, since each block, or procedure, of a computer program is an algorithm in itself, or a sequence of them.

Everyone who passed through the school learned algorithms, one of the first being the process of adding two whole numbers. But only those who studied in high school the "Briot-Ruffini algorithm", of dividing a polynomial by a binomial, early incorporated the term into their vocabulary. At more advanced points, students begin to call the process of numerical division of the third primary year "Euclid's division algorithm", but this is usually only for those who pursue a career in Exact Sciences. The fact is that most people get in touch with the word because of its use on the Internet.

And it is a sister word to another very familiar one: Algorism.

Both come from the name of a person, the medieval mathematician al-Khwarizmi, who worked at the House of Knowledge in Baghdad in the first half of the 9th century. The two words, algorism and algorithm, are attempts to pay homage to that important researcher, who formalized the Algebra of the equations and even created a process of solving the second degree equation - method of completing the perfect square, or method of al-Khowarizmi -, and other achievements.

When, therefore, users allow themselves to be taken by the suggestions presented on the screens of the portals of social networks or other applications, they are in the hands of the algorithms. They are very important instruments, as taxis also are. The user, when entering one of these vehicles, usually advises the driver on the route and destination. If he only knows the destination, leaves the choice of route to the driver. If it is an application-driven car, the machine is the one who suggests the path. In any case, if the citizen gets into the taxi without knowing where he is going and says only "go ahead", the driver will walk all over him. That's what the Internet portal does for you if you accept to stay in his hand.

Chapter 6. Virtual dating

In the last few centuries, many couples have been formed through dating by correspondence, that is, dating by letter, via mail. Romances have also appeared over the phone, but the standard was letters.

Operation. How was friendship by pen-pal?
The candidate for fiancé, or bride, published a small ad in a newspaper or magazine, with contact address, and waited at home for messages from suitors, those who fit the required profile.

A girl in a very small city, with little choice among the local boys, had the opportunity to get in touch with a large number of would-be boyfriends, whether from other small towns or from big cities. After a few exchanges of handwritten letters, and a few photographs, she made her choice. This worked better than if she simply accepted marriage to one of those few young men in town.

It is not that the city boys were not promising in any way. In many cases, she, or he, was going to study abroad, knew another large number of young people she could date, but she returned to the old ground and married someone from there. Intuition was behind this decision.

In the case of correspondence dating, they knew the other's personality through argumentation, calligraphy, physiognomy in the photos and, if there was a call in the meantime, also by voice. Finally, the face-to-face meeting was scheduled, they made up their minds, taking leave to wait for the result. If the correspondence died there, it was understood that the attempt was unsuccessful.

Woman. Which genre know how to choose the pair?
Man and woman always used intuition in making that choice, but the reasoned decision was in the woman's hand. In this universe of man-woman relationships, she has the domain of the future, as long as it is in her hand to act with autonomy.

The man who imposes himself on women in the decision to form a couple acts foolishly. Many do this because they have too much money or too much power. In these two cases, the man will never know whether the woman accepts his charge because she wants him as a person or because she is interested in his capital, unless in this field of money and power they are both in an equivalent situation.

While the man spent millennia at war, taking care of the collection of firewood and guaranteeing hunting and fishing to supply the house, the cave, the woman was taking care of the children, at home. She did not train intuition just to choose a husband, but mainly to choose the father of her children. She generates these in partnership with the man, but then carries them for nine months in the womb. Unconsciously, she chooses the sex and even the temper of the baby, among the millions of sperm that the man emits when ejaculating.

Research carried out in the United States at the end of the 20th century has shown that the choice that the egg makes over the sperm that will fertilize it is made by sending an electrical signal. Once that comrade was admitted to the embrace of the egg, this one closes off to the other millions of candidates. Obviously, in exceptional cases two sperm are accepted. And more rarely, even more than two. But the pattern is that of a single. In database language, we have a one-to-millions relationship case. Yes, the case of in vitro fertilization is beyond this type of natural regulation.

This electrical signal from the egg could be random, no doubt. But it is no exaggeration to suppose that the woman's unconscious has control over it. The unconscious, Freud says, is able to see through walls.

Language. Which genre is most skilled in language?

Physically, women and men are very similar individuals, distinguishing themselves only with regard to sexual development, with a greater difference in the genitalia, but also, in a more tenuous way, in the hips, shoulders and mammary glands, atrophied in men .

The most subtle difference is in the shape of the lips, coarse in the man and delicate in the woman. The main reason is the training of many millennia that the division of labor conferred on women, of teaching the rudiments of the spoken language to babies. This task, performed exemplarily for so long, is perhaps the explanation for the fact that few women have a deep voice. As she is the child's first language teacher, she has endeavored throughout our existence of Homo sapiens not to present a tone very different from that which babies feel to be closer to them and more reliable, which is the high-pitched sound.

There is a small fraction of women among feminists who do not admit that these determinant prehistoric differences between the two genders are pointed out. They are the type of people who prefer to live in self-deception.

The differences are great and in some ways they give significant advantages to women, while in others they give advantages to men.

If we think of activities like boxing, women are students of men. But if we think about language, whatever it is, men will always be apprentices. Women are the teachers.

Only those who did not pay attention to these details of the differences imagine that it was by chance that the inventor of the programming language was a woman, Ada Byron. And that the other phase of great steps was taken by Grace Murray Hopper, another woman, author of important theorems in this field.

Other women continue to develop programs and improve languages. And the female gender gains a lot in this when the education system is functioning properly. If the school is only serving to keep students, after precariously providing them literacy, then the struggle for spaces in society returns to the stage of natural selection, and in this case, the woman is a loser.

Influences. Who hinders the women's choices?

For language issues, women are more skilled and has more easiness to perceive. If we have to hire a language teacher for a child and we have to choose between a man and a woman, both having the same training and the same time of experience, there should be no doubt: the choice must fall on the woman, because her speech will be much more understandable to the learner. But women obviously have their shortcomings, and one of them is their susceptibility to being carried away by other people's influences.

Influence is a factor that opposes the enormous power of female intuition. A very common example is the mother's interference in the young woman's choices. The girl meets a boy and knows, analogically, that he is the man of her life. She has lived with him for weeks and has been able to confirm the information of his first impression. Now, her mother sees the boy once and did not have a good impression. One reason for this is that he threatens to steal her daughter.

The mother then proceeds to undermine the certainty that her daughter was already building. In addition to being the best friend, he is someone with at least two more decades of life experience. The daughter, contrary to her own feelings, yields to the mother's demands, and exchanges the boy for one that is pleasing to the family. The marriage may last a lifetime, but this daughter will never have the happiness she envisioned she would have with her previous boyfriend, demonized by her mother.

In many cases, when that daughter has something rebellious, the marriage takes place, but within a year or two she dismisses the imposed bridegroom, and returns to the boyfriend of her choice, if he is still available. It is something that hardly occurred in the 19th century, but which has become common since the end of the 20th century. As for the proportion of those who accept to remain in the marriage arranged by the mother, it is not possible to know, because research on this would face the barrier of the woman's reluctance to confess that she lives with a husband only by the mother's imposition. As the mother warns at the beginning that the daughter will accustom to the partner, this in fact occurs, and she will no longer be able to tell who was correct, whether she or her mother.

In addition to the interference of this type of mother, who tries to revive medieval customs in modern times, the marriages of convenience, the young woman also receives the influence of friends who are not relatives. As there is no hierarchy among non-consanguineous friendships, women's autonomy is greater in the face of interference from this type of medium.

However, it can be more subtle. Research from the 1970s showed that in a republic of girls, where, for example, four or more university students live, these young women have different dates for menstruation when they start to live together. After several months together, synchronization occurs. The one who exercises the strongest natural leadership maintains the date, but the others, who follow her command, adjust their periods for the leader's period.

If this influence occurs at the physiological level, it is difficult to deny that in the psychological field the facts are so.

Third. How can a man advise a woman?

For her decisions, in search of confirmation or dismantling of her impression obtained by intuition, the young woman can consult another woman, either mother or friend, or even a third element, which is the man, be he the father, be he a friend, and may be the priest, a schoolmate or a fellow worker.

In this universe, the man is really a third party, and, if he has a lot of experience and sharp eyesight, he will try to avoid giving hunch in the female choices when it comes to affective issues.

The priest serves as a bridge, and in that he plays a good role. In the Guarani Republic of the Missions, Clovis Lugon says, the young indigenous woman confided to the Jesuit confessor her desire to join a certain boy from the village. It was up to the priest to probe the intended. If he accepted the girl, the path was already paved. In case of irreducible denial, the Jesuit took the bad news to the girl, who tried to get the young man out of her head and go on to a second option. Respect for women's choice is implicit in this practice of the Missions. When the boy refused the girl, the community was not aware of it, because it was a matter of confessional. Otherwise, with acceptance, the principle of the woman's decision was valid.

In addition to this intermediary role played by the religious minister, it is also up to him to avoid the separation of the couple. For these actions, he receives efficient preparation in his training courses. And he knows, by intuition and experience (male intuition is respectable here), that separation with reconciliation involves a much greater risk than conflict that can be resolved within the home, without the limit of the break. Thus, if the woman realizes that her marriage is about to be broken and that is not in her interest, confessing to her religious minister and seeking support from him is the most recommended way. The minister, most likely, will call the husband of that faithful and, in conversations among three, try to minimize the motivation for the separation.

Reconciliation. Should a separated couple move back in together?

If it is a couple who have been living together for ten or more years and come to the dissolution of the contract, each going to a house, there will be no mistake in working for reconciliation. If both continue without contracting a new marriage, the tendency is to resume friendship and, who knows, even dating. But - attention! - it shouldn't go beyond dating. Even if the religious minister advises returning to the same roof, the most recommendable way, in fact, is to resist. Unless the man has undergone heart bypass surgery, it is advisable to avoid relapse into the emotions of life for two inside the same house (in this surgery, the connection between the heart and the brain is cut).

There are many reasons for not returning. If the woman got accustomed, for months or years, to live without her husband at home, accompanied only by her children, or anyone else, she could prove that she doesn't really need his presence. Currently the physical strength of the man is important alongside the woman to change the car tire, which will happen until a machine is invented that does this, or the culture of the car with tires is abandoned. If the house is single storey, the man is needed to change the broken tile, but it is not necessary when the residence is an apartment.

Equalization. Do modern machines empower women?

Returning to the tire changing machine, man must also realize that automated machines in general have eliminated the great advantage of physical strength that allowed the male gender to dominate the opposite sex in the early centuries of history. With the invention of the wheel and agricultural tools, man extended his power. The woman made herself submissive for millennia.

At the end of the 18th century everything started to change. The industrial revolution started to employ women and children, who had access to their wages. Women had access to literacy, which was previously restricted to men and some aristocratic women.

In a few more decades, women had access to their own machines, not just those in factories. The bicycle, the typewriter, the refrigerator, the train and the sewing machine came. Afterwards, these instruments gained electric versions, and also came the cake mixer, the blender and a large number of devices to help increase female power. The automobile, the plane, the crane and the machine gun entered the scene. None of these machines scares women, except when the tire has to be changed.

A woman driving a farm tractor produces as much as a man doing the same thing. Likewise, a woman driving a passenger bus or subway train provides the same service as a man.

If the woman still obeys the man and agrees to change her surname for that of her husband at the time of marriage at the registry office, maintaining the determinations of the Code of Hammurabi and the Napoleon Code, this is because she has not yet incorporated in her behavior the immense power that technology has brought her. From the 20th century, man must soak his beards. Not because he will suffer a rematch, but because he will have to learn to live with a partner who has already introduced the notion that she is not inferior to him.

Counselors. Is it fair to appeal to mothers in politics?

In the meantime, smart men have used women's reentry into social life in a less than loyal way, like a card up their sleeves. When a politician wants to defeat an opponent, or prevent him from ascending, he appeals to the mother of the person who would have the power to carry out the act.

Now, politicians are trained to resist the onslaught of opponents and to try to impose at any cost the position of their party or wing. But none of them are trained to resist a mother's request. As it is not in this area that female intuition is more keen, these unscrupulous politicians have increasingly taken advantage of this in an increasingly evident way.

A large number of women have an in-depth perception of political intricacies, but most are still building bridges to this new reality brought about by the Industrial Revolution.

Before monotheistic religions took over the world, it is a well-known fact that women held power. Men did battle and hunt, yes, but they were manipulated by the magic potions prepared by the ladies. These magic potions were a symbol, functioning much more as a representation than as a practical instrument. This is so true that the preaching of monotheistic religions against these practices was sufficient for unveiling them, as if the box of that magician who saw his companion on the stage had suddenly been made transparent.

In these millennia that followed, although there were queens in countries without Salic law, women's participation in politics was almost non-existent. In modern times, the first law authorizing the female vote was applied in 1899 in New Zealand. It can be said, therefore, that the re-training of women as a participant in political power issues dates from the beginning of the 20th century. A century, or a century and a half, seems to be a long time for a child, or even for a young person, but for the species, from a biologically superior branch of life, it is a tiny time. What is a century if we think about the time that has passed since the epoch when we descended into the trees and started to furnish our caves?

We look at the statues of the leaders of 2,000 years ago and see that their faces are the same as many of today's leaders. In our physical aspect nothing has changed, even though we have changed our clothing a lot. And if we find statues 50,000 years old, we will see that the faces are the same as today.

Our biological conformations have not changed since 250 thousand years, at least. We should not be under any illusions that our behaviors are introjected into our brain in just a matter of decades. We must not have Aristotle's illusion that "man is a political animal", that is, tailored for social life in cities. Although we have been in this way of life for 5,000 years before the Christian era, cities have not yet entered our blood. We have to learn urbanity at school, after having received more basic lessons from our parents, so that we can live with other citizens in a minimally civilized way. And it is no secret that a certain proportion of individuals, fortunately a very minority, never learn. They are the antisocials.

So, although men have a little more skill in politics, the advantages don't seem to be very great compared to women's skills. Within another century, or even less, any differences will disappear.

Women are excellent counselors on the issue of clothing, both male and female; in the decisions of microeconomics, that is, of family and company businesses; in speech issues; in health care; in matters of hygiene and aesthetics, among many other topics. Men can count on women in these fields, without any shame in asking for help when needed. Whoever asks mothers for help to overthrow opponents in the political life is the one who should feel ashamed of himself and others.

Disappointed. Is male political intuition very acute?

It was said above that men have some advantage in the use of intuition in political life because of some millennia of training in this field without the presence of women, who only resumed their participation in the early 20th century. However, it is necessary to stress that the advantage is very small. Seven thousand years in a 250,000-year trajectory of Homo sapiens culture is almost nothing.

Take an emblematic case. A country that went through a certain political turmoil then elected a national leader for an anti-liberal conservative line. It could be Honduras, Egypt or some other, it doesn't matter, because the stories are similar in the world of demagogy.

In that country, a public server who had done a great service to the country was enjoying enormous prominence, due to fortuitous circumstances that caused a problem to fall into his lap that demanded a solution for a long time. As he performed the task well, he became one of the most admired men of the nationality. He was invited to join the team of the new conservative leader. He accepted the call. At least half of the country realized that the choice would be very risky, but he nevertheless exonerated himself from his post of stable server and went to take office in the position of trust that was offered to him.

During the campaign, a well-known journalist who had lost her job at the company she worked for, due to financial problems that the house had been suffering, decided to run for deputy, lending unrestricted support to that conservative leader who would be elected.

Several politicians and public officials took the decision to profile with the leader, but these two cases, of the exemplary public server and the parliamentarian journalist, are a faithful portrait of how male intuition does not gain much from female in the political world. Historical time is too short for a man or woman to have incorporated considerable learning in this area.

After a few months in office, after the inauguration of the great leader, both the exemplary server and the journalist said they were disappointed, given the unpopular measures and the way the new boss treated all those under his command. The public server resigned from the position of trust, adding to the large list of unemployed. She, deputy, maintained her mandate, but became an opponent of the conservative anti-liberal leader.

Both the server and the journalist made the choice to support the leader using intuition, because with robust data and cold analysis they would never have worked to elect the disastrous boss. It should be remembered that in both cases the first contact with the major candidate was almost certainly in virtual mode. In politics, however, it is not that intuition does not help and should be discarded, but it cannot be taken as a guide when it is not built on consistent knowledge of the cause. Without this, the information asymmetry wins.

Instinct. Can instinct be trained in a generation?

When a psychologist, an administrator, a mathematician, or someone in a related field speaks of intuition, many find strange the meaning of the term. The reason is that most individuals, even the well-educated, confuse intuition with instinct, or at least think that the former has a lot of the latter.

They are properties of mind and behavior, but kinship does not go much beyond that. Let us see. Intuition is a concept of the theory of knowledge. By definition, it is the immediate understanding, or perception of something, without (conscious) interference from reasoning. Or, still, the ability to achieve this type of perception.

Instinct, in contrast, is a spontaneous, hereditary reaction, typical of animal behavior, used most of the time to favor the survival of the individual or his offspring.

No matter how much you study, think, train or debate, your instinct will not change, because it is innate. Intuition is much more than that. What is innate is the arsenal of physiological devices of the species and perhaps some more psychic resources inherited from the family, which is the subject of very recent research and which are therefore full of controversy.

However, studying, debating, observing, training, all this is an instrument for improving intuition. What you cannot do by instinct, you do by intuition.

A great chess player who thoughtlessly makes a move and this leads to a favorable result, is not playing with mere luck, but with intuition.

A well-prepared mathematician reads a problem and, before interpreting and modeling it, realizes whether he can solve it easily or not. It is his intuition that guarantees this, and it is hardly wrong.

Geographical. How does our memory portray the environment?

We sharp our intuition in analog mode. When we study Internet material we also learn things, obviously, but that's because we already have a base, which is being complemented. The process, however, is painful. The reason is that memory works on a geographic basis.

What does that mean? When you read a book and try to remember a passage from it, the first thing you do is to locate the position of the information within the text in your mind. If we remember the page number, which is rare, it will be even better, but what we try to do is to know if what we want to remember is near the end of the book, near the beginning or near the middle. This is how the data gets into the brain.

The teacher enters the classroom on the first day of the school year and learns that the student on the right, in the front desk, is called Peter, and that the student on the left, also in the front desk, is called Adriana. In the next class, three days later, if he has a good memory he will remember that on the right is the place of Peter and on the left, Adriana.

However, if in this second class he realizes that the students changed places, randomly, with a girl in the place where Pedro was and a boy in the place where Adriana was, he, no matter how much he looks at the faces of the students, will not identify who is Peter and who is Adriana. If he succeeds, it is because the two caught his attention in the first class. If, on the contrary, both are sitting in the same place as before, it will be very easy for the teacher to know that the one on the right is Peter and the girl on the left is Adriana.

Now, what happens with a text that goes up and down on the computer screen, or the smartphone? If the page containing important information is close to the end or close to the beginning, this is not configured in the mind, because there is no physical volume of sheets of paper in hand. There is the scrolling time of the screen, which can give an idea of the location, but this location is virtual, it does not say much to the brain.

To a learner who is studying for an entrance exam looking at the material on the screen, we should recommend to print the text and read it on paper. Learning is much more effective there.

Extension. Is photographing the person stealing his soul?

The Yanomami indigenous people, from the Brazil-Venezuela border, most of them being in Brazilian territory, when they had contact with the first white men in the early 20th century, soon discovered what the camera was for. It served to store and transport the image of people, and of the surrounding objects.

The first visitors coming from cities, who were the employees of theIPS, Indian Protection Service (now Funai, National Indian Foundation), and the soldiers of the border service, identified in the tribe's language the words *iaro* (hunting animals), *iai* (invisible beings from nature, or nameless beings) and *Yanomami* (humans), from the expression *Yanomami thepei*. Thus it was that the word Yanomami came to designate that people, in the same way that *Tupi* (people) designated in the 16th century the largest indigenous ethnic group in the country.

As an isolated tribe for almost a millennium, having returned to contact with other indigenous tribes only from the 18th century, the Yanomami have their own mythology, very rich in details. The origin of man is due to the mating between the demiurge *Omama* and the daughter of the water monster, called *Teperesíki*, lord of the cultivable plants. Omama's son became the first shaman of the tribe initiated there. Omama, creator of social and cultural rules, has a rebellious brother, *Ioasi*, responsible for the evils of the world and manipulator of death. The other peoples, including the whites (*napepei*: foreigners, or enemies), are also, with pertinence, creation of Omama. They are the result of a flood that took away the foam of the blood from the menstruation of former Yanomami women. This foam was eaten by alligators and otters, but even so, it was used by Omama to create people.

This whole culture contains knowledge that transcends the myths themselves, and is beyond all European science. Without ever having seen a camera, which was new even for the inhabitants of cities, they immediately translated the meaning of the act of photographing into their knowledge base. The photographer was simply stealing the subject's soul. What was inside that box, after the photograph was taken, was an extension of the soul.

Photography. Is light an abstract entity?

Photography is the register of light, according to the Greek etymology of the word. The great controversy about light was undone between the end of the 19th century and the beginning of the 20th century, by researchers such as willougby Smith (discovery of photoconductivity), Hertz (discovery of the photoelectric effect), Plank (formulation of the quanta theory), De Broglie (discovery of the wave nature of the electron) and Einstein (discovery of wave-particle duality).

The polemic had been installed when Newton's studies of the color disc and light scattering in the prism, at the end of the 17th century. Newton concluded that colors reach the eyes through particles, or corpuscles. Christiaan Huygens, a little older than Newton, did not give up his interpretation: Light is transmitted as a wave, not as a particle.

After centuries of fighting, Einstein ended the fight between supporters of both sides: Light is both a wave and a particle.

Albert Einstein: Light is wave of particles

Newton's discovery, the result of his intuition and deductions, since he did not have devices to visualize atoms, much less electrons, is what matters here.

This photograph that the Yanomami so feared was analog photography, called by many chemical photography (although the first digital machines were also chemical). In fact, the light emitted by the human face, through electrons, or photons, was captured inside the machine, to impress a cellulose film bathed in halogen silver crystals.

These natives knew what Newton also knew: the film, which will generate the photograph next, is marked by receiving particles emitted by the person, that is, it is part of the individual, carried away.

Mark. Do people of all ethnicities want to make their mark?

Wherever we go, we leave our mark. When we pile up some stones, forming a monument, abstract or figurative, it can remain there for centuries. Our work transcends our existence in this case. Or we can have the attitude of the Brazilian Indians: we leave nature as we found it when we were born. The maximum Tupi intervention of a lasting character in nature is the manufacture of ceramics, but this is because these people understand that in a few decades the baked clay utensils will be dissolved and reintegrated to the soil.

The ancient Greeks and Romans, differently, made a point of leaving their images immortalized in statues, caring little for what nature demands.

This cultural characteristic of not transcending one's existence in the natural world may be the explanation for this acute perception of the Yanomami regarding the theft of the soul through photography.

Now, an electron is just an electron, the reader may be thinking, very pertinently, in the fashion of Freud, who said in a lecture asked if the cigar he was smoking would not be a case of persistence of the oral phase: "Sometimes a cigar it's just a cigar". Yes, an electron alone can do almost nothing. It is a mere electrical charge of voltage only slightly greater than zero. But what the machine captures is not just an electron, it is not just a photon, but a set that forms an arrangement reproducing the person's physiognomy, through the darkroom that Leonardo Da Vinci created to use in his paintings.

However, perhaps those cautious sons of Omama did not notice the complete reversal of the phenomenon in the evolution of cameras. Neither they nor the children of the foam. Those photons that were transferred to the cellulose film, in its layer of silver salts, later revealed and passed to the paper, carried extensions of the subject's soul until this final stage, even when the printing was in a magazine or newspaper. In the modern digital camera, photons enter the lens in the same way as before, but from there everything is different: The information is transformed into pixels, which are processed digitally, that is, in terms of bits and "bytes".

The soul, the analog information that enters through the lens of the digital camera, goes out completely when the information that carries is transmuted to binary digits (bits). By the time of the click, the camera was receiving particles of the light emitted by the subject. They were his electrons and therefore were part of his soul. Converted into bits, these particles are dispensed, as they have already fulfilled their mission. In the digital photograph saved (kept) on the machine, there is no trace of the Yanomami's soul, nor of any other living being.

This is the digital world. Spooky? Our Yanomami brothers need to know this, because for them it is a source of relief.

For us in the big cities, the fact is frightening because our illusion that we were transported through our photographs now falls to the ground. If you kissed an analog photo of your girlfriend printed on paper, you were actually kissing the person, no matter how much, from her address, she didn't realize it.

When we kiss a printed digital photo, our lips find no trace of the photons originally emitted by the person in the portrait. They only find the digital representation, however much the resolution is much more precise.

Television. Has anything changed in the TV message?

Analog television has also been transformed into digital television. Radio has been going through this transformation, more slowly.

The relation of the photon transport is the same as that of the printed photograph. On analog television, if a video recorded in

VHS (*home video system*) was transmitted, what reached the viewer's screen were particles from the actors. If he was a candidate for elective political office speaking, he reached the voter, if not in body, at least in soul, that is, in photons, which were his, even if in the form of electrons inside a cathode ray tube. With digital television, the soul does not reach the viewer. Only a bit representation arrives.

The reader has already realized that the concept of soul used in this writing is that which was felt by the Yanomami and verified previously by Isaac Newton. It is not very related to the religious understanding of the word, because here the element is clearly materialistic. But this concept of the soul as a photon can certainly help theologians in their search for answers. In fact, scientists and others who work with this view have no doubt that, if there is a soul, it is a quantum entity.

There are great advantages in digital mode over analog. When a new politician grows in renown, he now does not need to spread his soul to win votes. He sends only a digital representation. It is the dream of all the old "shameless" politicians, who wanted to win the voter without giving themselves over to him.

There are also disadvantages. If a teacher teaches something through digital means, remotely, his soul does not reach the student. The student does not drink from the master that indispensable presence of true learning, the presence that the students of the Academy of Athens had of Plato when they walked through the gardens of the institution listening to the wise teachings of the philosopher geometer.

And the great disadvantage, which will be seen over time as an advantage, is that the honest politician, or the political indoctrinator of good will, does not reach the voter, or the one who is intended to indoctrinate, as a soul, but as something stripped of vital personality. The truth that depends on feeling for its transmission reaches the receiver when the communication mode is analog. It encounters an insurmountable barrier when the medium is digital. Those who are aware of this will laugh a lot when they see the despair of the canvassers trying to win fans on social networks. But the laughter will not last long when the person realizes that the result of the preaching is an increase in the strength of the obscurantists: The vote of those who do not want to know about party politics is caught in the loop by the politicians of the worst currents, a vote gathered by the naive ones who imagine convincing digitally. Steven Pinker, a noted evolutionary psychologist at Harvard University, has been alerting his peers to this phenomenon of reverse effect, but for now he has been preaching in the desert.

What excites the doctrine on social networks is the reception among those previously converted. When he posts, soon people of the same political line appear praising or expressing their agreement. This gives the illusion that his work is fruitful. It also appears, as expected, the reaction of those who have divergent thoughts. With the support of followers, the indoctrinator flares up, and recharges his batteries in the hope of converting yet another "pagan". Now, the one who reacts manifestly already has a defined position. It will not change via a digital preaching. And most of them, who do not say yes or no, but follow the discussion, if they do not have a defined position they tend to profile with the side that carries the most ignorance.

While returning to didactic activity, some friends of this author, such as Anchieta on TV Cultura in Sao Paulo, and Eliseu Gabriel, Wanda Estefania and Luiz Barco on TV Globo, among others, provided courses that were recorded on VHS and broadcast to the population. Their soul was spreading across the country. Other friends who now teach in the digital system of Univesp TV work with another type of relationship. It is not their photons that reach television students, but their digital representations, their pixels. Even your voice is transmitted only digitally, that is, encoded in bits at transmission and recoded, also in bits, at reception.

Conquered. Do you learn content on the Internet from scratch?
Despite the profusion of information available, learning through digital means is more painful. The citizen may think like this: My son was looking for the proof of a theorem on the Internet and, after a lot of research, he found it. He studied the theorem and understood the proof. So he learned. How can you say that one doesn't learn in digital mode? The answer is: One learns. But everything is limited to the universe that the apprentice has already conquered beforehand. If he was looking for the proof of a theorem, it was because he was already open to receive it. That

was not an epistemic leap in his life. Now let us take the example of a 20-year-old citizen, called Bellarminus, who never studied geometry at all and, therefore, although literate, has no idea what a segment, a polygon or the perpendicular straight line is. We persuade this individual to study on the Internet, with no analog teacher at any stage of the steps he will need to face. It should arrive, no matter how many months it takes, to understand and reproduce the demonstration of the *Pons Asinorum* (bridge of the donkeys), a basic theorem of application of congruence of triangles. The name Pons Asinorum came from the fact that in the traditional school, when the teenager learned that demonstration, he was jumping to the literate condition in Plane Euclidean Geometry, that is, he was leaving the donkey bridge. Anyone who bets, finally, on the success of the young Bellarminius' endeavor has at most one chance in two hundred million to win. If the reader did not know Pons Asinorum, it is the fault of the school program, which recklessly changed its priorities.

Another great advantage of digital photography over analogue, for those who believe that the art of voodoo, when used to do harm, has some tangible result - and this, if it occurs, is because of the action on the photons of the person, because about any rag doll the power of the wizard has to be very great - with a photo taken in digital mode, all the work of the needle skewering ceases to have any function. Sticking needles over the digital photography of John, Andrews or Sabrina, does not matter, because none of them is reached at a distance by this path.

Debates. Can analog conversations bring balance?

This book was digitally written. It arrives at the printer, as well as the virtual book processor, in digital form. It therefore runs the risk of drinking the poison for which it seeks to be the antidote, that is, the reader has been reached by digital means and may refuse to assimilate the facts reported here by reaching them through mere bits.

Apparently there is a dead end. But that is not it. The other side of the coin is the network of relationships. You, reader, is invited, at this very moment, to call people from your community to, analogously, discuss the ideas patiently linked here. Preferably, holding the printed book. If it is not possible, the virtual book also serves, because what counts are ideas.

"Author x says such a thing; I don't know if the conception makes sense ". The interlocutor who hears this will receive the information in analog mode, if what you have is a conversation not at the speed of light, but at the speed of sound, that is, an analog conversation.

Both debaters will be able to think more freely, one having received the information prepared digitally, the other, receiving it orally, without interfaces other than the air that separates them, in a friendly way.

It is clear that the reader who was open to apprehending the facts dealt with in this book, mainly about the notion of the interception of the quantum soul by digital processes, which prevents the sender from being in the place where he could have been using analog processes, this reader does not need to debate with other interlocutors, except to present these new conclusions.

However, the reticent reader, as well as the unbeliever, is urged to open the discussion with third parties. First of all, because he is not a refractory reader, because this one would not have reached the present chapter. The skeptical reader, this one, very unlike the refractory, if he started the book, he is reading these lines right now. So he needs to take advantage of this feature of the power to doubt and bring matters to the table.

Edges. What is a network of relationships?

The analog relationship, which through the emission of photons reaches people located remotely, has its strong version in the network of personal relationships, which takes into account only the strictly face-to-face contacts between individuals.

Computer Science has a subject-matter that addresses this issue, Graph Theory. A graph is the geometric representation of a network of relationships. It consists of only two elements, the vertex, or knot, and the edge. The first is the individual, human or not, represented by a tiny circle, while the edge, represented by a line segment, or any line, without interference or interruption, is the connection between two vertices.

A spider web is a type of graph, although the vertices are just the crossing of edges, without the black circles that we usually draw on paper, and the symmetries that we see there are nothing relevant to the theory. Another object related to a graph is a fishing net, whose vertices are quite accentuated, as they are the ties between the lines, which are the edges. Again, Graph Theory dispenses with any symmetries used in making this network.

In a network of relationships between humans, the degree of closeness between vertices matters a lot. If between one vertex and another there is only one edge, it is said that the person is in a handshake with the other, that is, they know each other personally. If between the vertex A and the vertex C there is the vertex B, meaning that there are two edges from A until reaching C, then A knows personally B and B knows C, but A does not necessarily know C personally, so the relationship between A and C is done, when necessary, through B. If between me and Flavia there are two vertices as minimum distance, which means that there are three edges, then I am three handshakes from Flavia.

A network of relationships may be representing a set of relationships in space, but also in time. For example, my father met the politician Joseph Maria, who I didn't know, but since I met my father personally, he is just a vertex between me and Joseph Maria, so I'm two handshakes from Joseph Maria, although he already be dead.

Jesus of Nazareth, as far as the New Testament accounts are reliable, established a network of relationships at the table of the Last Supper, asking that they share that bread in his memory. From one to another and from another to a third, from generation to generation, the request has been fulfilled for two millennia. This brotherhood includes Roman Catholics, Orthodox Catholics, Coptic Catholics, Anglican Episcopalians and Lutherans, as well as some other branches of Christendom. It is an immense network of relationships, which personally links today's Christian to the founder of the Christian religion. Supposing it was not Jesus of Nazareth, but some first-century priest, like Saint John of Patmos, the creator of that tradition, the network of relationships is present, linking Christians to this minister of antiquity.

For the purpose of this book, remembering networks of relationships that come from antiquity only serves to reinforce the concept, because what matters here are weak analog networks, connected by photons, and strong analog networks, these graphs of personal contacts that only take into account the relations in space, not in the time of successive generations.

Strangers. Who is a stranger in a network of relationships?

It is important to note that a person who is in your weak analog network, moving up a layer, starting to participate in the strong analog network, knowing you personally now, is someone who, although he did not look you in the eye before, face-to-face, he wasn't strange to you.

Montaigne takes good care of this when he writes, in the chapter Of Friendship, in his book Essays, about the day he met his great friend Étienne de La Boétie at a party: "We were looking for each other before we met in person (...)". He says that he knew the young poet through the reports of others and in writings that he had already read about him. And he continues: "In our first meeting (...) we found ourselves so close, so connected, so obliged to each other that nothing from then on was as close to us as we were from each other". It was not yet the time for photography, once the encounter took place between 1546 and 1548, but the extensions of the poet's soul spread through painted portraits, writings, and the vertices of the network, that is, close friends.

When they met for the first time, already knowing about each other, Montaigne and La Boétie were not strangers, for all intents and purposes.

Physicist Richard Feynman speculated about the air molecules we breathe and have always been around, in the atmosphere. At some point you breathed a molecule that passed through the lungs of Julius Caesar, or Jesus of Nazareth. If you visited the Louvre Museum in Paris and a few days later the pope did the same, it is almost certain that some molecule breathed by you also passed through the pontiff's lungs. In this way, one can imagine - Feynman did not go into that kind of detail - that all of us, the eight billion people on the face of the Earth, are known to each other, analogically. No, it is not true. Just as we share molecules on the breath, we also step on the same floors, sit on the same park benches and sometimes even drink water molecules that the other has already drunk. This confirms our status as brothers under the common trunk of the species, but it does not put us in the same analog network of relationships, strong or weak. The molecules that pass through our body are not part of us, and hardly take any part of us away. So, as much as you and the pope breathed the same molecule and attended the same museum, if no photograph of you reached him, if no writing of his own reached you, and if you two never had personal contact between you, then you and he are two strangers facing each other. But if you are a Catholic and by coincidence he, when a diocesan bishop, gave the ordination to the parish priest who gives you the host at Mass, then you are one handshake with him.

However, proximity to each other through a strong analog network and through a weak analog network are relationships of a different nature. Young Alice kisses the analog photograph of her favorite popular singer, whom she has never seen, nor knows anyone who has seen him in person. Another young woman, Beatrice, does not have a photograph of this singer, but she is friends with a classmate of his sister, in college, and is therefore two handshakes away from the artist. Who is closest to the singer's soul, young Alice or young Beatrice?

At the point in question, and according to the Yanomami belief, young Alice is closer, once she has part of the boy's soul with her. On the other hand, her network of relationships is weak, while Beatrice's is strong: young Beatrice can send a note at any time, and can receive something from the singer, or even have a face-to-face meeting with him.

Scams. Has the pandemic created friendships of digital origin?

We could write a collection of books larger than the old Encyclopaedia Britannica, which is no longer printed on paper, reporting already reported cases of women who were victims of Internet scammers. We don't need that much. It is worth mentioning some emblematic cases and you, reader, will see the dimension of the problem, if you have not yet convinced yourself of the seriousness of the original digital relationships. The original relationships are distinguished from those that are digital, but that are the consequence of analog relationships.

During the quarantine of Covid-2, in the first half of 2020, one of the resources to make bearable, and even fun, the confinement of families in their homes, was virtual relationships. Through social networks, by video conference or by e-mail, people remained connected, telling anecdotes, informing friends about the news, discussing the virus itself and, unfortunately, sharing the pain for loved ones killed in the pandemic.

These quarantine relationships were strengthened if their origin was analog. Friends who were only virtual remained in the same situation as before, without much deepening. And, lacking the presence of analog friends, Internet users look for them, avoiding new relationships.

Salvador. How did happen the 10,000 BRL scam in Bahia?

Two women from Salvador, Bahia, according to the newspaper O Globo, on November 21, 2019, echoing a story on TV Bahia, fell into the so-called "love coup", and lost almost R$ 10,000.

The first victim, 52, met on the Internet a citizen who claimed to be called "Daniel", a resident of Denver, United States, and who made frequent trips to Brazil. She was enchanted by Daniel's kindness, and allowed herself to be involved in him in less than a month.

Finally, Daniel warned that he would be coming to Brazil again and would send some gifts to her, through a carrier. Days later she received a call from the alleged carrier saying that she must deposit a certain amount so that the product was released. She did that. Then there was another call saying that there was a sum of money in that box she would receive and that it was against the law, so that if she didn't deposit R$ 8,500 to the carrier, she would be reported to the Federal Police and would have to face major problems.

When she tried to contact Daniel, already suspicious of being a victim of a coup, she saw that he had blocked her. She made a debt of R$ 4,350 with a loan shark to pay part of the expense with that carrier. He managed to pay R$ 1,000 and owed R$ 3,350. When she complained to the police station, she said that they thought she was joking and did not give much importance to the complaint.

The second case, told in the same article, is about a 45-year-old woman, mother of three adult sons and who was looking for loving contacts on a relationship portal. There were three months of virtual interaction, which included promises of marriage. Finally, the scammer claimed to have sent a suitcase and, because it was stuck in customs, the victim would have to make deposits. In the transactions she lost R $7,500, according to a complaint she later made to the police station. "Any human being with hopes gets involved", the woman said. "The words, the promises, the beautiful things (...), I even started to call him my love".

Macapá. Are women victims of men only?

Another story was told by the BBC News Brasil portal, on February 27, 2019. "I accepted to marry someone who did not exist" was the title of the article.

Nurse Luana, 30, who lives in Macapá, Amapá, met a boy who claimed to be called "Alvarus", 35, through a relationship app. Recently approved public defender, he said he was born in Rio Grande do Sul and a few weeks ago he moved to Macapá. "I believed everything he said to me; I didn't look for information about him because I was very delighted with his attitudes towards me ", reported Luana. The boy sent a bouquet of flowers by an emissary, who handed it to Luana at her workplace. Shortly afterwards, over the Internet, he asked if she liked the gift, and asked her to date. She accepted.

Always using excuses to avoid the face-to-face meeting, one day he asked her to marry him, and she also accepted this new request. This coup was not very expensive, since Luana's disbursement was R$ 600, to cover an urgent loan request by Álvarus.

With the case reported to the police, investigations revealed that the person responsible for the profile was a 24-year-old girl from Macapá, who had already deceived dozens of women in that city.

Rio. Do women risk suffering injury?

A third report deals with a case that became well known because of television coverage. Told in the magazine Veja of April 18, 2019 (in 2020, the coronavirus prevented the repetition of this type of occurrence), we have the most brutal case, which occurred with the businesswoman Eliane Caparroz, 55 years old. After eight months of digital relationship with the lawyer Vinícius Batista Serra, whom she met virtually on a social network, she agreed to make an appointment, and then invited him to dinner at her apartment on Saturday, April 16.

As they both had virtual friends in common, which is a plan

widely used by the bad guys in the net, she felt at ease and confident to sleep on his lap after dinner. She woke up in the middle of the night while being brutally assaulted by Vinicius. "The torture session lasted about four hours, according to the victim's brother (Rogerio Peres Caparroz)", Veja reports.

He cursed, bit and punched the victim, when her screams caught the attention of porters and neighbors. When they entered the apartment, they found Elaine unconscious. Vinicius had escaped, but was intercepted at the entrance, and soon the police arrived, taking him prisoner.

The victim was admitted to the ICU of the Hospital Casa de Portugal to treat severe fractures of the face and arms, and trauma to the kidneys and lungs.

Unlike the two previous cases, this was not a financial scam story. Vinicius confessed to having woken up in an "outbreak", after sleeping under drunkenness of wine.

Women looking for Internet dating are thus at risk of falling into the hands of both criminals and psychopaths, as well as people with more acute mental disorders.

Paulista. Can a woman alone hit a man?

The unfortunate outcome in a relationship of digital origin that most shocked Brazil and even neighboring countries did not occur with a woman as a victim, but a man, in a crime committed by his partner.

Exame magazine published, in the November 29, 2016 edition, an interview with the victim's brother, based on an article in the newspaper O Estado de Sao Paulo, which followed the trial of the case in court. Reporters had to design scenes for the trial, including photographic evidence, once the court did not allow recording by photographs or broadcast on TV.

Marcos Kitano Matsunaga, the murdered husband, on May 19, 2012, met his partner, Elize, in 2004, on an accompanying portal. In a few weeks he fell in love with her, and, in order to marry, he asked for a divorce from his wife. He was a successful businessman, heir and chief executive officer of the Yoki food industry, highly known for several decades.

Before the tragedy, it appears that the only person to have suspicion of Elize was the reverend who officiated the marriage between her and Marcos. He warned the businessman to keep under control the arms store he kept at home, because she was weakened and could do something silly. Marcos, however, trusted his new wife too much, and was not affected by the religious minister's warning.

According to his brother, Mauro Kitano Matsunaga, Elize told Marcos' family that he had gathered some clothes in a suitcase, took about R$ 15,000 and called a taxi, without saying where he was going. As he did not return, she said she believed he was missing. She told Mauro that the building's cameras should have a record of his departure, but after much tracking, nothing was found about it.

She also showed Mauro the footage taken by a detective she hired to prove suspicions that Marcos was seeing another woman. He said he was surprised by this attitude at a time like this, when the family was experiencing growing anguish at the disappearance of his brother. It was then that he received an email from Marcos saying: "Tell mom and Elize that I'm fine; I can't talk now."

The family filed a complaint with the police, who went on to investigate the businessman's whereabouts.

It was later learned that she knew the password for Marcos' email service and she was the one who had sent that message.

Days later Mauro was called to the MLC in Cotia, Greater Sao Paulo, to see if a head found in the forest was his brother's. To confirm, Mauro asked to see the victim's hands and feet, and soon he no longer had any doubt that he was his brother.

Taken as a suspect, she later confessed she was the perpetrator of the murder. Lawyer, she also had a nursing technician course. She shot her husband at point-blank range, cut him up and took him to the woods, in pieces, in suitcases.

Questioning. Is not the risk in analog mode the same?

Advancing the questions, there is no doubt that these facts could have occurred without the Internet participation. A scammer could approach an alleged victim on the street, or even seek contact by phone. A man could also look for an accompanying by phone at an agency. And these people would be at risk, apparently in the same way. This "in the same way", itself, is not consistent with reality. Victims have always existed since Abel, killed by Cain, but the villain has always had to face the intuition of the one who would be harmed. Under the new virtual world, a woman's intuition is impaired, but a man's intuition is also damaged.

The number of men who marry, or cohabit, with women they met in the brothel is large. One should not look for statistics on this because a very small number of men confess that their wife was a call girl. The boy goes to the house of tolerance, looks in the girls' eyes, knows their story, and his intuition, without any fantasy, helps him choose one, opting for one that has already chosen him without his realizing it. Many bowds participate in this referral, inclusive serving as guarantors of the relationship. And how many are the cases of wives of that origin who murdered their husbands? They are certainly not numerous or notorious, if they exist.

Project. Does everyone have a life project?

The other side of the story, which should be intriguing the reader's mind right now, is the fact that many digitally formed couples work.

Badly compared, an individual decided to commit suicide by practicing Russian roulette with a 38 caliber revolver. His plan was to fire a single shot. If he hit the bullet, with a sixth chance, he would be dead. With five-sixth chances, he would survive. If he fired and stayed in those five sixths, he is a survivor, and his life from this moment is a probabilistic fact (in theory, because, as already said, Freud wrote that the unconscious sees through walls - which occurs in analog, but not digital cases, something that the father of psychoanalysis did not live to see).

Most people have an unconscious life plan. Some of them put this on paper, bringing to the conscious level what was hidden from them. Few people do this about writing their life project because, since we were children, we discovered that our plans almost always depend on external factors. Because of this, we prudently scaled our plan B, and our projects become a tree of possibilities.

Once this case of people who design a life project without a tree of possibilities occurs in a negligible number, let us stay with the two common types, those who have projects unconsciously formulated and those who have no project, but go on living according to the circumstances and without anguish over the difficult choices they have to make. Which number is greater, that of those who have an unconscious project or those who have no project at all? As the thing is unconscious really, in both cases, we bet on those without a project as being the largest number.

For these people, driven by the circumstances, without any relevant personal project - it is not worth following the herd, because that is not an individualized life project - it does not matter whether the person finds the spouse on an Internet portal or at a party at a friend's house. These people do not value or instruct their intuition. Thus, it is important that the pair to be found is a beautiful person, be seen for the first time in digital photography, or in a face-to-face meeting. Whether the couple formed will be a case of success or not, this does not depend on the mode of origin, whether virtual or analog.

It is important to note that the unconsciously constructed life plan follows the same process as the instruction of intuition. If you train your intuition, at the same time you forge your life project.

Dangers. Can we know how intuitive we are?

In the midst of the great amount of benefits brought to humanity by the Internet, the risks it carries are also great and very serious. It is about them that we have to draw attention in these times when the digital world has been reaching every home on the planet.

We can identify the dangers listed below.

    1 - "Soulless" quantum contacts in relationships;
    2 - Impossibility of using intuition in choices;
    3 - Bad elements diluting in anonymity;
    4 - Profusion of false news;
    5 - Videos in "deepfake".

The central point in the change in the perception of human beings with the arrival of the digital world is the disabling of the efficiency of intuition in the choices of friends, electoral candidates, employees and spouses. If, on a first contact, eye to eye, the owner of a well-trained intuition, for example an experienced human resources professional, had a high degree of assurance that he discarded the less promising candidates and selected the most appropriate ones, with physiognomies analysis made initially through Internet all that training is no longer worthwhile. This professional chooses with the same power as anyone who has never selected candidates before.

As is well known, intuition is not a measurable thing, at least until now. Tests were developed to measure mathematical knowledge (since antiquity), to assess the intellectual quotient (IQ), to assess emotional intelligence, to measure the degree of alcohol in the body through breath (breathalyzer), to classify blood type and to calculate cholesterol levels. As for intuition, it is not yet known how to measure. The reader can find methods out there that guarantee to calculate it, but it is misleading. What one does is a kind of measure of emotional intelligence, nothing more. In reality, the ability to resist voluntary impulses is measured, and this is not intuition, it is more related to the degree of resilience or stoicism.

After a few years of free Internet activity, with the harm already known, several types of precautions have been taken to alert users and at the same time reduce damage. One of the initiatives is the creation of the Sleeping Gyants group, which works to identify and denounce the financing, mainly through advertising, and most of the time in good faith, of portals of false news and anti-liberal preaching by part of large and reputable companies. These companies, once alerted, cut the source of funds. This is one of the fronts, but we know that this is still very little. Even with the pandemic, scams that do not involve expectation of face-to-face meetings continued to exist. The users themselves should be the firsts to receive guidance on how to act in this new world of siren singing.

Clairvoyance. How to control our brain frequencies?

It is no secret to anyone, and it does not involve any mysticism, the art of using the unconscious to obtain information that the conscious vigil cannot capture. One can, for example, make the mind go down to the alpha level of perception, which is an condition obtained with relaxation training and the search for individual peace, reaching a mental situation very close to that of sleep. It is the reduction in the intensity of the mental frequency that provides the alpha level with greater perception capacity than the one we have at the beta level (frequency above 15 Hertz, or 15 cycles per second), which is the conscious wakefulness.

With lower frequencies than those of the alpha level (7 to 14 Hertz), we have the theta level (less than 7 Hertz), of deep sleep, and the delta level (less than 4 Hertz), of very deep sleep, or coma.

When we are trying to solve a difficult mathematical problem, even if we are concentrated on the details of the statement, the key, the "insight", appears at the moment when we let the mind to relax. With all that data spinning around in the brain, trying to match the formulas that are known to us, the brain tends to increase its frequency. But at a certain point we allow the confidence we have in our mastery of the subject to come into play. We relax and let the unconscious work without pressing it. Sometimes, in this mental work, we think about our girlfriend (girls think about boyfriends), we remember a bucolic walk or a trip to the pizzeria with friends, all to give the unconscious a break. Then we think about the problem we are solving, but without paying attention to details about it, so that we don't get back to the starting point. That's where the solution comes in: The details are configured again, but with the aspect of the issue resolved. We return from the alpha level to the beta level, bringing a gain.

Professionals who study the human brain have recommendations for anyone who wants to achieve the alpha stage, enjoying its benefits. The first step is to sit, or lie down, comfortably, if possible listening to relaxing music; this done, the second step is to breathe slowly and deeply; the third step is to relax the body, limb by limb. The final act of the process is to let the feeling overlap the reasoning. It is three or four minutes until the alpha level arrives.

It seems somewhat difficult to suspend reasoning while one is awake, but it is not so. It is not difficult because we are accustomed to doing this daily, when we close our eyes to sleep. If we are thinking, if we are reasoning, we are necessarily trying to solve a problem, be it academic, be it our daily and prosaic life. For example, that neighbor insists on borrowing money. How will it be possible to be free of this harassment? If this is the last problem we are trying to solve when we close our eyes to sleep, the moment it leaves our mind, we fall asleep. On the contrary, when we have insomnia, we jump from problem to problem, which brings great anguish to those who suffer from this disorder. Yes, you can be on watch without, however, solving a problem. It's true, but right now you are just remembering.

Hypnosis. Can we guess under hypnosis?

Hypnosis is practiced with the patient taken to the theta level of mental frequency. If he is sleeping and at the same time talking, interacting with the hypnotist, he can reveal facts that his beta level of brain activity does not allow to see. Many kidnapping cases have been cleared up with people being hypnotized and revealing in detail the place where the kidnapper was being held.

A hypnotized patient, with well-trained intuition, can find out, for example, which candidate will win a particular election, if the procedures are analog. If the campaign had more weight in the digital mode, if the voters choose their candidates for information obtained digitally, then the unconscious of that hypnotized person cannot scrutinize anything.

No other method of divination that used the power of the unconscious has more function in the digital world. The limits of tarot, coffee grounds, bibliomancy, I Ching, auguries (interpretation of the flight of birds) and premonitory dreams are all in the analog world. In the field of the Internet, no prerogative of the unconscious prevails.

Thus, whoever wants to do psychoanalysis through virtual conversations, through social networks, will be trying to get milk out of stone, to use a very old image of unproductivity.

Whether it is a good thing or not the impenetrability of the contents of the cloud by the unconscious is something to evaluate with time. What must be established now is that we have two different worlds in front of our old brain: the analog world and the digital world.

For many activities, the digital world is better and, in some cases, irreplaceable. For other activities, the best thing is to be limited to our palpable analog world.

Care. Are there any precautions we should recommend?

The Internet user must, therefore, provide himself with some basic care, so that he does not sin due to unforeseen circumstances.

1 - Do not choose a spouse of first virtual contact;

2 – Do not vote for a candidate known virtually;

3 - Do not hire employees by virtual contact;

4 - Do not rely on news from an unverifiable source;

5 - Do not make political or religious preaching on the Internet.

Knowledgeable. Should the man choose his spouse?

Those in a hurry who throw themselves thoughtlessly at the proposals offered virtually need to think of the example of an unsuspected person in the digital world: Bill Gates. He, who enriched himself with the production and trade of computer programs, was the richest man in the world when he married Melinda Gates.

If he had intended to find a woman in the cloud, very many thousands of candidates would surely appear. Rich and famous, how would he know if the woman chosen from among them would even deserve deference? The best attitude was not to take any chances.

Steve Ballmer, his old partner at Microsoft, made the bridge. Bill Gates should marry his own secretary, Melinda, is what he said to his friend. He was the closest person, who helped him at all hours, and who liked him.

Now, nobody needs to ask Ballmer if he did that without previous conversations with Melinda, because conversations are certain.

So there are two possibilities: He perceived her marital interest in Gates, which was a silent message, or she missed out on a conversation with him who did not have the boss as a mere friend, or as a mere boss. In either possibility, it was Melinda who chose. And Bill Gates was right to have signed below. There are decades passed by a couple who share the same concerns and perspectives.

Now let us imagine the situation of a powerful man who "chooses" his wife. Among the various suitors, he hit the hammer: She is the one.

If she didn't choose him, or if she went after him just for being rich and famous, she will have the option to pretend, in sexual acts, that she has a lot of affinity. This is not convincing. The woman who really chose the man conveys the message by pheromones, not by gestures or words. As much as we think that pheromones are hormones used only by irrational animals, they are behind the happy and lasting relationships between human couples.

That man who thinks he has chosen will hardly have a happy married life. And she, the chosen woman, will have a mediocre emotional life alongside her magnate.

He may think that if she chooses well by his female intuition, he may likewise choose well by his intuition as a man. He thinks wrong. Male intuition is important and powerful, but when it comes to forming a couple, it is the female intuition that must be respected. She releases an egg every 28 days, in a stock of about 400, while the man releases many millions of spermatozoids per week. In this biological question, she has to be very careful. And she is, in fact.

However, if the choice is not made in analog mode, but in digital mode, then anything goes. *Allea jacta est.*

Cacildo Marques

@cacildo